Luigi Pizzamiglio

Distributing co-operative societies

An essay on social economy

Luigi Pizzamiglio

Distributing co-operative societies
An essay on social economy

ISBN/EAN: 9783744723459

Printed in Europe, USA, Canada, Australia, Japan

Cover: Foto ©Suzi / pixelio.de

More available books at **www.hansebooks.com**

[*AUTHORIZED TRANSLATION.*]

DISTRIBUTING
CO-OPERATIVE SOCIETIES

AN ESSAY ON SOCIAL ECONOMY

BY

Dr. LUIGI PIZZAMIGLIO

"The distributive society touches no man's fortune, it seeks no plunder; it causes no disturbance in society; it gives no trouble to statesmen; it enters into no secret associations; it envies no dignity, it subverts no order. It means self-help, and such share of the common competence as labour should earn or thought can win."—Holyoake, *History of Co-operation in England*, London, 1879.

"Whoever can teach the masses of the people how to get five cents' worth a day more comfort or force out of the food which each one consumes, will add to their productive power what would equal a thousand million dollars a year."—Andrews, *Institutes of Economics*, Boston, 1889.

LONDON:

SWAN SONNENSCHEIN & CO.

PATERNOSTER SQUARE

1891

To the UNIONE COOPERATIVA *of Milan,*
Which, overcoming wide prejudices,
Gloriously carried into effect the principles of Rochdale,
Showing to Italy
In Distributing Co-operative Societies
An abundant source
Of moral and economic blessing.

PREFACE

I DESIRE to return, so far as I am able, publicly, my warmest thanks to the distinguished Professor Luigi Cossa—on whose advice I publish this extremely modest study—who, with high-minded liberality, placed his rich library at my disposal, and procured for me the most recent books; and to my friend, Dr. Federico Guasti, a most zealous and able co-operator, who, besides allowing me access to the library of the Milan *Unione Cooperativa*, favoured me with the notes which he had compiled in 1886 on the occasion of his writing a theme for his doctor's degree, and which he published only in part, and furnished me with very important information on the co-operative movement of to-day. Also I sincerely thank my friend, Cavaliere Vittorio Ceresa, Secretary to the Minister of War, who gave me a full account of the *Unione Militare*, and all those friends and well-wishers who assisted in procuring for me recent notices and books, without which my work would have been sadly incomplete, or rather entirely so; for, if any value is to be found in it, it consists in the patient and exact compilation of a great quantity of data and notices.

In excuse for the defects—not a few, it may be—of this work, I can only adduce long study of, and great love for, my theme, which I chose for my dissertation in taking my doctor's degree this year at Padua. For the rest the reader—whose full indulgence I feel that I must crave—will see that I have studied co-operative societies without senseless misgivings or rhetorical enthusiasm, without finding them the panacea for all social ills or the Utopia of visionaries, without taking a purely doctrinaire or simply practical line of treatment, and that I have been inspired by the exact and scientific idea of co-operation maintained in the Pavia school, from which have proceeded able co-operators like Gobbo, Guasti, Manfredi, and Rabbeno, and by the hopeful words of Professor E. Vidari, according to whom "any one who despairs of co-operation shows that he has small faith in progress and that eternal and fateful law of transformation, which even the most stubborn wills in vain attempt to evade."

L. PIZZAMIGLIO.

BIBLIOGRAPHY.

—:o:—

E. Raoux, *Des sociétés mutuelles de consommation*, Lausanne, 1858.
E. Pfeiffer, *Die Consumvereine*, Stuttgart, 1865.
G. Birait, *Des sociétés coopératives*, Narbonne, 1866.
J. Duval, *Des sociétés coopératives de consommation*, Paris, 1866.
P. Bernabé, *Las sociedades cooperativas*, Valencia, 1867.
F. Reitlinger, *Les sociétés coopératives en Allemagne*, Paris, 1867.
Eu. Richter, *Die Consumvereine*, Berlin, 1867.
J. Holyoake, *The History of Co-operation in Rochdale*, London, 1867.
N. Benard, *Les boulangeries coopératives*, Paris, 1868.
Em. Nazzani, *Le associazioni cooperative* (in the *Industriale romagnolo*), Forli, 1868-1869.
F. Schneider, *Anweisung für Consumvereine*, Berlin, 1869.
J. Simon, *Le travail*, Paris, 1870.
Schulze-Delitzsch, *Die Entwickelung des Genossenschaftswesens in Deutschland*, Berlin, 1870.
J. Holyoake, *The History of Co-operation in England*, London, 1875-1879.
A. Roulliet, *Des associations coopératives de consommation*, Paris, 1876.
E. Martuscelli, *Le società di mutuo soccorso e cooperative*, Florence, 1876.
E. Brelay, *Les sociétés de consommation et les banques populaires*, Paris, 1881.
F. Schneider, *Taschenbuch für Consumvereine*, Leipzig, 1883.
Newton, *Coöperative Distribution* (in the *North American Review*, vol. ii., 1883).
Hubert-Valleroux, *Les associations cooperatives en France et à l'étranger*, Paris, 1884.
E. Brelay, *Les sociétés coopératives*, Paris, 1884.
L. Buffoli, *Le società cooperative di consumo*, Milan, 1885.
U. Rabbeno, *La cooperazione in Inghilterra*, Milan, 1885.

C. Casella, *Una questione vitale per le società cooperative di consumo*, Caserta.

U. Rabbeno, *La cooperazione in Italia*, Milan, 1886.

E. Pasquali, *Le società cooperative e la tassa di minuta vendita*, Turin, 1886.

M. Guala, *La cooperazione e il dazio consumo*, Vercelli, 1886.

Shaw, *Co-operation in a Western City* (Minneapolis). Published by the *American Economic Association*, 1886.

A. Warner, *Three Phases of Coöperation in the West*. Published by the *American Economic Association*, 1887.

C. Lagasse, *Les sociétés coopératives*, Paris, 1887.

A. Maffi, *Previdenza e Cooperazione*, Rome, 1888.

E. Pasquali, *Le società cooperative in rapporto alle tassa di dazio consumo e di minuta vendita*, Milan, 1889.

L. Ponti, *Manuale pratico amministrativo per le società cooperative di consumo*, Milan, 1889.

Delaruelle, *La question sociale réduite à une simple question de boutique*, Valenciennes, 1889.

A. Labadini, *Il forno rurale cooperativo*, Rome, 1889.

U. Rabbeno, *Le società cooperative di produzione*, Milan, 1889.

G. Patrignani, *Le associazioni cooperative di consumo*, Bologna, 1889.

Schulze-Delitzsch, Schneider, Schenk, *Jahresberichte für 1880-1888 über die auf Selbsthülfe gegründeten deutschen Erwerbs und Wirtschaftsgenossenschaften*, Leipzig u. Berlin, 1881-1889.

Co-operative Wholesale Societies' Annual, Manchester, 1888, 1889, 1890.

Il primo, il secondo and *il terzo congresso dei cooperatori italiani*. Official report of the Committee of the Federation of Italian Co-operative Societies, Milan, 1887, 1888, and 1889.

L. Bodio, *Le associazioni cooperative in Italia*, statistical report, Rome, 1890.

The most recent numbers of the economic and co-operative journals and reviews, Italian and foreign.

CONTENTS.

	Page
DEDICATION - - - -	vii
PREFACE - - - - - -	ix
BIBLIOGRAPHY - - - - - -	xi
Chapter I. Idea of Distributing Co-operative Societies -	1
,, II. Importance of Distributing Co-operative Societies - - - - -	9
,, III. Conditions and Limitations of Distributing Co-operative Societies - - -	32
,, IV. Different Forms of Distributing Co-operative Societies - - - - -	43
,, V. Some Questions relative to the carrying on of Distributing Co-operative Societies -	55
(a) Whether one ought to sell on credit -	ib.
(b) Whether the distribution of goods ought to be made at the lowest prices or at the current market prices - -	64
(c) On selling to non-members and their participation in the profits - -	88
(d) How the capital is formed and the profits distributed - - -	98

		Page
Chapter VI. Spread of Distributing Co-operative Societies		
	England	111
	Germany	125
	France	132
	Italy	138
	Switzerland	150
	Belgium	153
	Denmark	156
	Sweden and Norway	157
	Holland	158
	Austria-Hungary	159
	United States	159
Chapter VII. Relations between Distributing and Manufacturing Co-operative Societies		167
,, VIII. Some Observations on the Theory of Co-operation		177

CO-OPERATIVE SOCIETIES.

CHAPTER I.

IDEA OF DISTRIBUTING CO-OPERATIVE SOCIETIES.

ONE evening in November, 1843, a dozen poor flannel weavers of Rochdale, a small city near Manchester, having met together to devise some remedy for their desolation and misery, aggravated by a recent crisis, in a simple observation struck out the fruitful germ of distributing co-operative societies. "Many persons," they observed, "grow rich by selling to us what we need retail. Clearly, therefore, something sticks to their fingers—something is withheld in their interest, so that they are enriched at our expense. Why not ourselves become rich by banding together to buy the goods they sell us, wholesale?"

The carrying out of this idea, glory of the Rochdale weavers, was precisely what gave rise to distributing societies, which have as their office, "to buy genuine articles in common use wholesale, in order to sell them to members retail, procuring for the latter the economic advantages of collective consumption without the moral drawbacks of living in common."

The chief merit of the "honest pioneers" of Rochdale, who opened up the way to a new form of association, consists in their having found out a means of saving without any sacrifice or lessening the sum of enjoyments which those weavers were accustomed to procure with their scanty pay. To be able to save, it is necessary to have an income exceeding the outlay required to satisfy the needs of existence, in which condition only too small a proportion of working-men are found, to whom it would be well-nigh cruelty to recommend the depriving themselves of something, or saving, in order to better their condition. Saving *on* the outlay, on the contrary, which has been rendered possible by co-operative societies, in contradistinction to saving *in* the outlay *(épargne par la dépense),* is attainable by every class of society, being merely the result of an improvement in the *technique* of distribution.

Since saving—whether it be considered subjectively as abstinence, or as an effect of economic progress—is always obviously distinct from growing rich at other people's expense,[1] no one can say that he is injured by

[1] Voltaire's opinion, extended to individuals and every social combination, by which " un pays ne peut gagner sans qu' un

GENERAL IDEA.

distributing societies. And neither, therefore, can it be said that distributing societies aim at injuring other retail dealers: the natural slowness of these societies in developing, and the serious difficulties of their extension in many branches of commerce, leave the few who *are* injured easy means of employing their energies elsewhere. And it is weak, though disinterested, sentimentalism to oppose distributing societies out of regard for small traders, since no one has guaranteed to them that they shall sell exclusively, or in perpetuity, and no one can honestly oppose an institution which confers a notable advantage on the many with a doubtful loss to the few. Or, must railways and the printing-press, because they have injured carriers and copyists, be deemed injurious to society? As to that, distributing societies ought to be welcomed, in addition to other reasons, because they help to keep down the excessive number of small traders, which, like all professions which do not call for manual labour and involve direct production, tends constantly to increase.[1]

autre perde" and "telle est la condition humaine que souhaiter la grandeur de son pays c'est souhaiter du mal a ses voisons" has been proved false, in that it is not necessary that the economic gain of one individual should be attended by the commensurate loss of another (Domela-Nieuwenhuis, *Das Sparen*, Halle, 1889).

[1] J. S. Mill used to maintain that it was possible to dispense with $\frac{9}{10}$ of the English dealers: T. Rogers believed this of at

The distributing society does not aim either at enriching itself to the detriment of consumers. Rather it has been formed by them and for their benefit, and, therefore, can have no object in speculating, *i.e.*, in preparing products and services in order to offer them to those who have need of them, and gain on the compensation; and, not aiming at gains, it can never be seduced, as happens sometimes among traders, through excessive covetousness, to adulterations or cheating of any kind.

But if distributing societies have no speculative object, neither do they propose to offer their loans gratuitously. The idea of co-operation is based on individual amelioration co-ordinate with that of other individuals, not on the principle of one bearing the other's burden or making sacrifices for other people's good : the co-operator is on a par with, and not in any wise subject to, those with whom he co-operates, and the familiar term " self-help," which means just helping oneself in harmony with the interest of the community, expresses most vividly the idea of co-operation. It is still frequently the practice, however, to speak of distributing co-operative as benefit societies, and there are founded among us under this title in-

least $\frac{4}{5}$; in England failures in retail trade amount to about 40 millions sterling annually. The number of retail dealers is excessive in Prussia also. See Roscher *Nationalökonomie des Handels und Gewerbfleisses*, vol. iii, Stuttgart, 1887.

stitutions which have only the name of co-operative societies.[1]

How may a distributing society be defined ?

A satisfying, precise, and complete definition of these societies was given only this year by Dr. Emilio Cossa, whereby "distributing co-operative societies are associations for the purchase or production on joint-account of objects of consumption."[2]

By this definition the difference is clearly delineated between distributing societies and co-operative manufacturing societies. Some persons used to think that whenever the distributing society did not limit itself to buying goods wholesale in order to sell them again retail, but imported some modification into the nature of the goods purchased, it ought to be considered as a mixed distributing and manufacturing society; and this confusion proceeded so far that a distributing society was called "mixed" only for employing a workman to break up "loaves" of sugar which, in the nature of things, cannot be distributed retail whole.

It appears to me that distributing co-operative

---

[1] Here is a recent example. A society calling itself distributing co-operative was established at Terni in October, 1889, among the *personnel* of the great bakehouses, foundries, and steel factories, evidently for the sole object of benevolence since it pays no interest on the capital and sells commodities at cost price *plus* working expenses.

[2] *Primi elementi di economia agraria*, Milano, 1890.

societies may, indeed, devote themselves to the manufacture of one and all of the goods on sale, but, so long as they act in regard to the manufacture like any monied investor, and their office is that of procuring for consumers a saving on the expenditure, they cannot be identified with manufacturing societies formed by "workmen and artisans who, putting together their labour and capital, commence business, assuming all the risks of production in order to enjoy the entire profit thereof." Co-operative bakehouses, for example, which store and work grain in order to distribute it in the shape of flour or bread, cannot be considered manufacturing societies, because they exist for the sole behoof of consumers, the more so as the workmen employed in them are generally paid hands simply.

Distributing societies are, however, sometimes confounded with other forms of co-operation.

Co-operative farming syndicates which have as their office to purchase seeds, manure, sulphur, etc., wholesale, and sell them again to their own agriculturist members; and, generally, all societies which buy raw materials wholesale in order to sell again to members exercising the same profession (*Rohstoffgenossenschaften*), and those which charter or buy machines to be used alternately (*Werkgenossenschaften*), cannot, though exercising a distributive function, be properly considered distributing co-operative. The societies, in fact, are associations of rich manufacturers

GENERAL IDEA.

for procuring for production more favourable conditions than each can obtain individually; their business, therefore, is to favour producers, not consumers.[1]

[1] In practice there is sometimes observed between distributing societies and farming syndicates a conflict of interests, by which the difference indicated (often forgotten by those who look merely to the mode of operations and not to the object of these unions) between the two forms of co-operation is rendered more evident. It is, in fact, obvious, that when farming syndicates, besides distributing goods to members, sell their products, it is for their interest to keep the selling prices high in order to gain as much as possible; while distributing societies are interested in buying at the lowest prices in order to benefit consumers.

This conflict, however, is not to be deemed irreconcilable; distributing societies purchasing by means of syndicates directly from producers at current prices always save more than by applying to some wholesale trader; and producers, on the other hand, finding a certain market in distributing societies, can dispense with wholesale traders and grant some abatement without suffering by it. A fresh instance of such agreements is related by Fougerousse in his *Coopérateurs Français*, published this year.

Two co-operative slaughter-houses at Lyons have partially succeeded in removing all intervention between producers and consumers by buying live cattle from farming syndicates and dividing the net profits between the purveyors, *i.e.*, the syndicates and their patrons. It is easy to understand the operation. 300 francs, for example, was paid for an ox; this has produced 425 francs through the meat, and 25 through the remainder (hide, fat, horns, hoofs); the general expenses of all kinds, amounted, let us say, to 100 francs. That gives a net gain of 50 francs, which is spread over the total of the buying and selling price (300 + 425) or 725 francs. The net gain is, therefore, some 6·90. Thus, 6·90 per cent. of the 300 francs goes to the

In like manner joint-cellars which aim at increasing and perfecting the production of wine, even when, as is often the case at the outset of these societies, they limit themselves to renting a store where the products of members are collected in order to sell them on their own account and with the profits of the assortment, thus procuring some of the advantages of large enterprises—like every *Magazingenossenschaft*, generally—cannot be held distributing societies, since their object is always to increase the value of the product, to favour, therefore, production, not consumption.

No doubt, joint dairies are manufacturing societies, notwithstanding that the manufacture is *sui generis*.[1]

Cossa's excellent definition absolves me from entering into other particulars, since to me the idea of distributing co-operative societies seems adequately and securely delineated.

purveyors, 6·90 per cent. to the consumers. The common expenses, which are borne by the producer and consumer, are those of transport, workmen for slaughtering, etc., the carrying on of the concern, and the interest at 4 per cent. on the capital employed. All may purchase at the co-operative slaughter-houses at Lyons, and compete for the profits on consumption. Prices of meat are the same as at other butchers' shops in the same quarter. During the first three months of its existence (October, November, December, 1889), the two slaughter-houses have distributed for consumption more than 92,000 francs' worth of meat, and including hides, the sale has risen to more than 100,000 francs.

[1] N. Rabbeno *Le Società cooperative di produzione*, p. 10, Milano, 1889.

CHAPTER II.

IMPORTANCE OF DISTRIBUTING CO-OPERATIVE SOCIETIES.

SERIOUS objections are urged to the importance of these societies.

It is a vital question for distributing societies whether, in taking the place of the retail trader, they really effect some economy, or whether, on the contrary, the difference in the wholesale and retail prices does not precisely answer to compensation for those expenses which every retail dealer, whether an individual or a society, must inevitably bear, *i.e.*, advances of the buying price, payment of rent for the stores and shop, wages of those who assist in the working of this industry, etc.

Cernuschi and Leroy-Beaulieu opposed distributing societies on this ground. Cernuschi gave judgment thus: "All that exists in economic, as in physical and mechanical, life is absolutely necessary, and, therefore, it is a mistake to think of abolishing middle-men," and he recommended, "*ne vous en prenez pas à vos voisins les plus utiles, les intermediaires.*" Leroy-

Beaulieu observed: "The belief that co-operative societies can succeed is a prejudice due to a double illusion: it is thought that middle-men obtain enormous benefits, without, as it were, doing anything... Many have believed that it would be advantageous to suppress intermediaries between producers and consumers. They would like to do away with those low trades which have as their object the storing and distributing to the entire population, all over the country, of articles necessary for daily life. If the force of circumstances, superior to men's fancy, had not prevented it, these trades would have been supplanted by a crowd of anonymous microscopical societies without capital, competence, or responsibility; and in the meantime the least reflection would have sufficed to prove, that there is no industry carried on with so few wheels or with so much economy as this retail trade, the object of contempt to those above, of jealousy to those below, and of the calumnies of all." And carried away by an eagerness, which abroad it is the fashion to dub Italian, Leroy-Beaulieu asserted: "All the latest information teaches us that the co-operative movement has been checked, and that distributing societies are very far from being numerous and prosperous." Further on I shall show how ill-informed was the author who has been cited, and who certainly spoke in good faith, with regard to the co-operative movement.

For truth's sake it is needful to mention that later on[1] Leroy-Beaulieu disowned his opinions of 1872 respecting the necessity of numerous small intermediaries, constituting himself the champion of large warehouses, and showing the advantages of the concentration of trade. "From the moment," he concludes, "that the diminution of intermediaries is a relief to society, we ought not to hesitate in preferring the good of the latter to the prosperity of the former."

The criticism of Cernuschi, the *un*converted adversary of co-operation, is based on the exaggeration of the co-operative idea. Contempt for retail traders, a relic of ancient opinions,[2] and the imprudent and inaccurate declaration, on the part of some co-operators, of a wish to abolish them, have determined, perhaps, Cernuschi's exaggerated opposition.

[1] *Essai sur la répartition des richesses*, Paris, 1881.
[2] καπηλεύω signifies to sell retail and to falsify, and the difference in Greek between κάπηλος and ἔμπορος is well known. At Rome contempt for retail traders was no less accentuated (Cicero, *nihil proficiunt mercatores nisi mentiantur : mercatura, si tenuis, sordida putanda est*), a contempt which was reinforced in the Middle Ages and sanctioned in the prohibition, inscribed in the *Corpus Juris canonici*, against buying in order to sell again at a higher price, an action considered a grave sin, because it gained money without adequate toil. "Barullo" and "treccone," synonymes of retail dealer, much used among us, expressly indicate a very vile occupation carried on with covetousness and a tendency io cheat. The word "rivenditore" (retail dealer) also is not without blemish ; in the carnival songs we read : "*Noi siam ben rivenditori—Ma di bella roba e buona.*"

It is important, therefore, to inquire whether it is really an illusion that middlemen obtain enormous benefits.

It cannot be denied that the retail trader exercises a useful economic function by exempting the consumer from the necessity of furnishing himself at his own risk with every object he requires, of laying out a considerable capital, in order to get provisions wholesale and store them at his own risk and expense. Only, it is asked whether for the services rendered them by retail dealers consumers do not pay a price greater by a long way than their cost.

To this demand it has been replied *à priori* that in a market where competition is unrestricted, it is impossible that there should be excessive gains.

This observation, which is oftener made in regard to wholesale trade, loses a great part of its value in the case of retail trade, in which there are not many buyers and sellers on the same 'Change, with every facility for comparing, directly and at the same time, the demands of different sellers. A retail buyer cannot compare at the same time, and without great inconvenience, the price asked for a commodity with that demanded elsewhere by others for the same commodity and since it is impossible to choose, he prefers trusting to the modesty of the vendor's demand to verifying in regard to each purchase the price paid in other shops. Moreover, the habit of buyers always to make purchases in given shops, even if things are sold at lower prices in some other shop, the common prejudice that he who sells cheaper offers worse goods, and the wish to avoid the trouble and loss of time consequent on making long rounds in order to change shop and obtain a doubtful and, perhaps, trifling save, bring about a kind of local monopoly which favours the excessive growth of profits and serves to explain the fact that, in spite of the reduction on many goods wholesale, no corresponding abatement is observed in the retail prices.

Competition in retail is, therefore, much less efficacious than in wholesale trade; and nothing but the fear lest an extraordinary gain should be found out by the purchaser and induce him to betake himself to other shops, can restrain the covetousness of retail dealers, who find it extremely easy to make capital out of the ignorance of the consumer concerning the state of the market; an ignorance very rare among buyers and sellers wholesale. More than that, competition, when active, may sometimes reduce the profits of vendors without any advantage to consumers: the multiplication of shops and the division of custom may operate in such a way that each person, selling at an equal price, may sell in smaller quantity. If, then, the retail dealer should choose to seek compensation for this lessening of profits in some forbidden means, there would result from this competition rather an injury than an advantage to the consumer.

The fact that the prices retail do not move parallel with the wholesale prices does not altogether settle the question whether the difference in the two prices is not excessive.

Statistical researches, such as would permit a trustworthy reply to this question, are still wanting, and were only recently entered upon by the advice of the German "Society for Politico-social Studies" (*Verein für Socialpolitik*).

In a sitting held at Bonn in November, 1887, this society proposed, among many others, these two enquiries:—

1st, What is the relation between the wholesale prices at which goods are bought from producers, and the retail prices at which they are sold to consumers?

2nd, Does the difference in the prices, on the given hypothesis, seem excessive or only a fair remuneration for the services rendered by the distributive agencies?

The first work which has attempted to reply to these enquiries is a painstaking monograph of Van der Borght on the trade of Aix-la-Chapelle.[1] In this large and careful work which may be called the first example[2] of such researches, Borght replies to the

---

[1] *Der Einfluss des Zwischenhandels auf die Preise auf Grund der Preisentwicklung im aachener Kleinhandel*, Leipzig, 1888.

[2] Before it short and special articles had been written in Con-

second enquiry formulated by the *Verein für Social politik* that "on the part of the retail traders there is no excessive gain."

Borght's reply, however, does not correspond with the result at which one may arrive on examining the data which he has himself collected. The reader may judge for himself from the following view, taken from p. 252, which shows the average surcharge of retail dealers on the price of 46 different objects from 1878 to 1886.

In the case of 3 articles the rise was from 10 to 15 per cent.
,,   8   ,,   ,,   15 ,, 20   ,,
,,   9   ,,   ,,   20 ,, 25   ,,
,,   7   ,,   ,,   30 ,, 40   ,,
,,   1   ,,   ,,   50 ,, 60   ,,
,,   1   ,,   ,,   100 ,, 150 ,,
,,   1   ,,   ,,   150 ,, 200 ,,

Can even those who wish to examine these data with much partiality say, that an increment reaching to 100% is not immoderate?

Van der Borght reckons farther on (p. 264 *et seq.*), that in 1886 a family of eight persons at Aix-la-Chapelle must have paid into the coffers of retail

rad's Jahrbücher by Dr. Hirschberg, *Zur Statistik der Roggen- und Brodpreise in Deutschland;* by Scheel, *Zur Statistik der Brodpreise in Deutschland;* and Dr. Scharling, *der Detailhandel und die Waarenpreise.* Scharling's writing concerns only the trade in Copenhagen, and is rather theoretical than practical, especially from the paucity of data.

traders about 35 marks for colonial goods, and adds:—
"This amount is so small for a large family that it would hardly be decent to wish to save it by going direct to wholesale traders or producers." It seems to me that if a family succeeded in saving 43 *lire* a year on the use of colonial, and an equal amount on other articles, the total amount would not be trifling even for those who had no need to save the *centesimo*.

After Borght's monograph there were published in Germany four short studies on this subject[1] (besides the discussion held about them at the general congress of the *Verein für Socialpolitik* at Frankfort on the Main in 1888[2]), of which I think it profitable to give an account from their importance as regards my theme.

The first of these studies is that of A. Bayerdörffer and has for its title:—*The Influence of Retail Trade on Prices at Madgebury;* the second that of O. Gerlach:—*How the Price of Meat is formed at Halle;* the third, that of L. Wolf, studies:—*The Price of Bread in Leipsic in 1885;* the last, by W. Lexis, has to do with:—*The Distributing Co-operative Society*

---

[1] These works are found in the collection, *Untersuchungen über den Einfluss der distributiven Gewerbe auf die Preise*, Leipzig, 1888.

[2] *Verhandlungen der am 28 und 29 September, 1888, in Frankfurt a.m. angehaltenen General—Versammlung des Vereins für Socialpolitik*, Leipzig, 1889.

in *Breslau and the Prices of Retail Trade.* Of these the works of Gerlach and Lexis are the most noteworthy.

Gerlach arrives at the conclusion that the great reduction there has been of late years in the price of beasts of slaughter is not met with in that of meat, and that no sign of competition is perceived among butchers; only an improvement, very perceptible in the last decades, is noticed in the quality of meat, whereby butchers seek to attract customers.

Lexis says that the average gain of retail dealers cannot be termed excessive at Breslau, but that, taking all together, for the services of these dealers an outlay occurs, which, economically, may be considered as an excessive luxury. In fact, the most usual competition consists in procuring for buyers the greatest possible conveniencies: carrying goods to the house, despatching parcels, keeping up the shop with a certain pride, etc.; all advantages implying expenses for the retailer which are subsequently paid for by the consumer.

Prof. Conrad, however, upon examining the works of Borght and Bayerdörffer, in a report presented to the congress above mentioned, manifested the fear that the rise in prices owing to retail trade was really excessive; and the *Verein für Socialpolitik* immediately advised the continuation of these studies, especially as regards the price of meat and bread.

B

From these painstaking German works, based upon observations gathered only in particular cities, and with respect to particular objects of consumption, there certainly cannot be deduced a trustworthy and general law, if only because the agreement between the results of these researches is not complete, nay, rather, from Conrad's words and the unanimous approval of his words by the congress, the conviction seems rooted in German economists that traders make an inordinate profit out of consumers.

French economists, less scrupulous with regard to figures, have easily calculated the average gain of these dealers. Reclus, in order to show the usefulness of distributing co-operative societies, calculates that wholesale purchase is exempt from the surcharge of about 33%, which burdens retail traffic, *i.e.*, he writes, "if 100 kilograms of a commodity cost 3000 francs retail, wholesale they will cost only 2000 francs." Michel Chevalier, approximating to Reclus' calculation, estimates the gain of retail dealers at 35%. With greater exactness Cochin, in an enquiry made in 1866, indicated the amount of the savings effected by a society which had set up a store for the sale of clothes, eatables and firing, as :—45% on wood, 66% on sausages, 56% on potatoes, 62% on vinegar, 127% on *jambon fumé*, 33% on wine, 55% on cotton coverings, etc.

The usefulness of distributing co-operative societies

appears, better than from these uncertain and incomplete calculations, from the results hitherto obtained. Distributing societies are no longer an experiment, but a success: and suffice it to mention here, among the data to which I shall refer later on, the eighty million *lire* which are annually saved by English co-operative societies taking the place of traders; and the calculation made by Neale, according to which these societies, if they distributed the savings as dividends on the capital, would be able to give on an average from 50 to 100%. Similarly, the Breslau Society, according to Lexis, would be able to give 87% on the capital.

The distributing co-operative society in fact always saves the profits of the trader, not always small, and it may obtain greater, since it is in some respects better off than the trader. Thus the expenditure required in order to attract and keep certain custom, and uncertain knowledge of their customers' needs, which causes them to risk long storages with possible deteriorations, are unfavourable conditions for traders, and conditions in which it is not usual to find distributing societies, which have an assured body of customers with needs approximately determined. Further, ready-money payment, which is the essential and fundamental principle of distributing co-operative societies, cannot be applied by retail dealers: the customer is not offended if credit is refused him in the society;

whereas the shopkeeper, by refusing credit, seems to show a lack of confidence in the customer; so that on that account, from the very beginning, the trader finds it convenient to sell, in exceptional cases, on trust, and the exception speedily becomes the rule. While the shopkeeper is thus compelled to raise the price of goods in order to find compensation for the risk inherent in credit, the distributing society finds an easier and safer means of saving in ready-money sale.[1] Moreover, distributing societies have the advantage, as compared with small dealers, of purchasing in larger quantities, and therefore nearer to producers, and generally find in their members greater patience and indulgence for any inconvenience which may arise, than the shopkeeper in his customers.

On the grounds stated, I think it may be maintained that by means of distributing societies a saving is certainly obtained in favour of consumers, although this is of very varying extent.

A fresh objection was made to distributing societies in a congress held at London last September, by Mr. Haddleton, a trades' unionist, who denied their importance because "in the end they only take money out of one pocket and put it into another."

But, pray, is it exactly true that the present distribution of wealth is the best possible, and that the complaints of workmen and the suffering masses,

---

[1] Of ready-money sale, I treat more in full in the sequel.

against the immoderate enrichment of certain individuals at the expense and through the toils of others, are wholly unjust? Besides, Haddleton's remark is inaccurate, because distributing societies only wish to prevent money, hardly gained with great labour and toil by the workmen, from coming out of the consumer's pocket for the benefit of a useless trader.

The advantages which may be derived from distributing societies are various and manifold.

With regard to social economy, as a whole, it is observed that the consumer, who saves by means of these societies, is able considerably to improve his own condition, either by increasing his consumption or hoarding what he has saved.

On the first hypothesis, which must be verified in practice (since it is impossible but that some consumers should feel the need of increasing quantitatively the consumption of certain goods, or of consuming new), there is in the market a greater demand for goods, corresponding to the consumer's increased purchasing power, such as to diminish the evils arising from over-production, which depends, perhaps, not so much on the lack of consumers, as on the production being too dear in proportion to the consumer's means. Further, many middlemen, abandoning trade, would be able to devote themselves to production, and thus cause the price of those goods, which they previously raised by their intervention, to be lowered.

The increase then in exchanges, arising from new purchases, would favour a larger development of trade, and a wider application of the division of labour.

In practice these results will be the more considerable the greater intensively and extensively the saving obtained: it is certain, however, that, owing to the difficulties and limitations of distributing societies, there cannot be anticipated from them a new golden age in economic life.

Incomparably greater and more direct advantages for workmen are derived from those societies which enable members to accumulate small savings and offer a safe employment of capital, thus powerfully promoting habits of prudence and thrift, without which there can be no lasting improvement in the working classes.[1]

Furthermore, distributing societies are justly considered as an efficacious means for neutralising those agreements between traders for imposing artificially high prices on the market which in Southern Italy are considered as a form of "camorra,"[2] and which are

[1] I deal in a special manner with this sort of society further on.

[2] Here is an instance related by a correspondent of the *Perseveranza* in a letter from Palermo, the 17th of November, 1879: "Grain, before it is converted into bread and pastry,

widely diffused in Italy and abroad, in so much that our municipalities have often been compelled to place restrictions on them by re-establishing "calmieri,"[1] mediæval institutions.

There was a wish also to oppose the distributing society to all those associations of producers which aim at dominating the market and regulating its prices, and which are widely diffused in the United States under the name of "pools" and "trusts." There, sometimes by secret agreement or without constituting legal societies, they have succeeded in artificially raising the prices, and have obtained from the State

must pass through various kinds of 'camorra,' which Government, notwithstanding constant efforts, has never succeeded in destroying. This 'camorra,' from time immemorial, has taken the name of *posa* and this is what it consists in. There is the society of brokers, of waggoners, of sifters, of millers, of bakers, and, finally, of pastry cooks. Every one of these societies has taken upon itself the obligation of maintaining those individuals of their class who are in want of employment; and, therefore, they claim, and there must be dealt to them, payment which is not in proportion to the labour furnished by them, but to the persons, including those who do not work, who must live on that pay. That is why, in Palermo, labour is so much more costly than in every other Italian city. Add to this a municipal rate on flour which exceeds, by authorisation of Government, the maximum fixed by the law, and you will have explained why bread is sold at 64 *centesimi* and pastry at 84 *centesimi* the kilogram."

[1] At Pavia, in 1889, the Municipality found the "calmieri" on bread unnecessary, and abolished it in consequence of baking co-operative societies.

some monopoly or concession, which forms the ambition of every American manufacturer, whose characteristic it is "ever to keep an eye open on the patent office."[1] In France[2] and in England these associations are called syndicates or rings; and in Germany, also, since 1873, there have been formed *Cartels*, associations of great manufacturers, which fix the lowest price, below which no member of the Cartels can sell.[3] In Russia, too, there are instances of similar associations; indeed, the council of ministers approved of a project, presented by certain Russian factories, called *normirofka*, which was to fix the price of sugar, but to which the Czar refused his sanction.

But for a long time yet the best protection of consumers against these societies will be in foreign competition only, since, as yet, the time does not appear

---

[1] The *Standard Oil Trust*, founded in 1882, with 70,000,000 dollars, which had a capital, at the end of 1889, of 90,000,000 dollars, owes its marvellous development to the railway tariffs established by it.

[2] The Deputy Lacour - Grandmaison, in a sitting of the Chamber, the 23rd March, 1886, referred to the *Consortium*, a syndicate of Paris refiners, which claims in a sovereign manner to regulate the price of sugar, and which had so much influence that while at Marseille, where the syndicate had encountered opposition, 95 francs were paid for sugar, 100 and 101 were paid at Paris.

[3] See Claude Jannet, *La Socialisme d'Etat et la réforme sociale*, Paris, 1890.

to be approaching in which distributing societies may successfully contend against these agreements, usually most powerful.

One indirect advantage, which extends to all consumers, is the turn given to competition in retail trade: it has been noticed that where co-operative societies are instituted, the habits of retail dealers undergo a change, the petty traders being compelled to abstain, in order to withstand the competition, from the adulteration of articles and frauds in weight and measure habitual to them. The same thing happens in the case of wholesale trade, where the co-operative society does not lessen the competition between producers or wholesale traders by wishing always to purchase on the best terms, but improves it, because by renouncing any further dealings with any one who may have deceived it only once on the nature or weight of a commodity, and by making known to other co-operative societies the dishonest firm, it renders every deception seriously hurtful to the dishonest trader, and introduces loyalty and honesty into trade.

Distributing societies never have any motive for deceiving people as to the quantity or quality of goods. Whoever considers the constant progress in the art of adulterating and falsifying, and the difficulty, which has naturally grown, of discovering adulterations without long and intricate analyses, will be easily persuaded that the arrangements of the penal codes (cod. ital. art., 319 et seq. and art. 295, art. 42 sanitary law), or the care of hygienic societies or public testing institutions, of which there was a melancholy instance last year at Paris, are insufficient for the sure protection of consumers: where many innkeepers with a few bunches of grapes quench the thirst of, and intoxicate, thousands of topers, and the flesh of tainted carcases of asses and mules is eaten as pork, one can only hail distributing societies as a providential means for the public safety.

Every one knows how wide-spread is the practice of cheating on the weight and measure, as well as on the quality, of goods, and it is useless to insist on this argument: only by way of curiosity I quote in a note[1]

---

[1] At Farczyn, near Warsaw, some dozens of persons lately presented symptoms of poisoning due to the adulterations to which flour is subjected in order to increase the weight, there being added to it some kind of herb capable of being ground, such as darnel, horse radish, not to speak of the 10·50 per cent. of a mixture of barley and rye, etc. (p. 44).

Drs. Bulowski and Alexander analysed more than forty sorts of tea, varying in price and origin: adulteration is enormously wide-spread. First of all there is the sale of tea already used: then comes the addition of leaves of *epilobium angustifolium*, then adulteration with other substituted vegetables, and finally sophistication with mineral substances (p. 44).

At Hyères, in the south of France, the poisoning was ascertained of a great number of persons by adulterated wine. The inquest showed that the accidents were due to the introduction of a certain quantity of arsenic mixed with wine decocted the from the *Journal* of the Royal Italian Hygienic Society (1st January 1889) some historical evidence culled from a dispensary taken at random, and I recall how that in England it has been found necessary to establish an "Anti-adulteration Association," which publishes the *Anti-adulteration Review* " in order to show consumers the snares laid for their health by unscrupulous and worthless traders."

But the intellectual and moral advantages of distributing societies cannot be passed over, since their high ideal is to co-operate in that social well-being, which can have a solid foundation only in a sure intellectual and moral progress.

It is impossible, writes Fawcett,[1] to exaggerate the educational value of co-operative societies on the working classes. A workman who has a few pounds invested in a distributing society soon comprehends the true function of capital, and instead of regarding capital as a mysterious agent created to oppress labour, is persuaded that capital, no less than labour,

second time, in order to hinder its fermentation. Eleven corpses were examined of persons presumed to have died in consequence of this poisoning, and the experts, after proceeding to analyze the bowels of the corpses themselves, confirmed the suspicion, and the judicial authorities condemned the guilty person (p. 46).

Declamations are unavailing: but does not an institution which can save the lives of many persons deserve only for this reason to be highly appreciated ?

[1] *Labour and Wages*, London, 1884.

is essential to industry, and is entitled therefore to proper respect.

Only in cases where the people can save something, do men feel an interest in maintaining the great principles which are fundamental to the existence of society; otherwise they regard them with indifference and aversion, and the smallest motive suffices for their deciding to attack them. If those who are hungry cannot practise virtue, those who possess something feel all respect for the property of others; and distributing societies inspire and diffuse this respect.

The moral and educational advantage is splendidly illustrated by an article in this year's *Co-operative News*. The workman who has only to take account of his own wages, is at a distance from business, lives by himself, has a whole world closed to him and does not know the chief rules of trade. No sooner does he become a member of a co-operative society and attend the meetings, than he acquires, almost without knowing it, a new set of business notions. The effect is much greater in the case of those who take part in the administration: these accustom themselves to commercial operations, and increase their sense of responsibility yet more, from the knowledge that they act on behalf of their comrades. This is the real compensation of the administrators, who work hard and usually receive meagre remuneration. But it is not necessary, in order to enjoy the advantage of those lessons which co-operation imparts, to have a share in the administration. The monthly, quarterly, and yearly meetings afford every opportunity for gaining new information and going deeper into that already gained. How many members, says the article, understood the mysteries of a balance-sheet before they became co-operators? Some of us, perhaps, cannot give a full account of it now. In any case every member, whenever he wishes, has complete facilities for becoming expert in this difficult subject. If he is doubtful on some point, he has only to make it a question for the next meeting. Few hours can be so instructive, in a business sense, as the sharp criticism to which the balance-sheet is usually subjected.

Among the moral advantages must be reckoned the stimulus to temperance, which is derived from the abolition of sale on credit, and which diffuses the habit of saving, which is, says Rocher, as it were, that virtue of thrift which is equally remote from idleness and avarice, since it is the daughter of prudence, the sister of temperance, and the mother of independence. Therefore many English co-operators, belonging to the working-classes, are abstainers (members of temperance societies, *teetotalers*), and certainly drunkenness, which is always a great evil, is considerably lessened by distributing societies.

Co-operative societies thus help to solve the so-called social question. Ferdinand Lassalle used to preach that a solution of the social question could be found only in the universal diffusion and application of tendencies to association. But neither through individual initiative nor State intervention can these tendencies be at the same time diffused and applied; whereas, distributing societies, the easiest and simplest form of co-operation, can, by showing the advantages of association and inspiring confidence in it, prepare the minds of the people and be a school for more difficult and complex forms. Especially in the case of us Italians a wide and successful application of these co-operative societies might weaken that distrust and suspicion of every form of association, and educate and correct that excessive freedom from restraint on the part of individuals, which is, as Turiello says, the common root of all the special defects of the Italian character.

The material and moral advantages which have been pointed out and which are yet inconsiderable in comparison with those due to particular systems of organisation, if they cannot form a complete picture of the small and manifold effects, direct and indirect, which these societies spread through the entire social organism, and which are the more important the more slowly, and, as it were, unconsciously, they are produced, nevertheless show clearly what blindness and what unjust hatred has inspired the verdict, promulgated by certain traders of Berlin and supported by several German chambers of commerce, that "co-operative societies are harmful and dangerous experiments for the good of the State and of society."

CHAPTER III.

CONDITIONS AND LIMITATIONS OF DISTRIBUTING CO-OPERATIVE SOCIETIES.

THEORETICALLY, in the case of retail trade the co-operative form would appear the most obvious, and that which ought to arise before the speculative form. In practice, however, the speculative form develops itself and prevails over the co-operative; since many persons or families experience common needs before an association arises to satisfy them, it is needful to convince people of the desirability of establishing a joint-store, to fight against their customs and dislike of innovations at a great risk of discords and friction: meanwhile, some clever person thinks of setting up a shop and satisfying those needs, and at the same time receiving compensation for himself: the shopkeeper has had no need to play the apostle, and all have found it advantageous to have recourse to him. When, however, consumers become aware of the splendid gains and frauds of traders, they are easily persuaded of the desirability of a joint-store, and then distributing societies arise.

Distributing societies have thus arisen, like every institution destined to last, by reason of *real* needs, not needs artificially created or exaggerated by the apostles of co-operation, who confine themselves to making known the means of providing for those real needs and indicating how those means can be most usefully applied: it is needful to prepare every reform step by step, awakening a consciousness of their importance in the public mind, and ordering institutions in such a way, that that consciousness may gradually discover a way of developing these institutions: and this, and only this, is the task of the apostles of co-operation.

Since these needs are not felt by all consumers with equal intensity, a very great diversity is observable in the quality of the members and in the spread of these societies. To-day more than ever the need of distributing societies is felt by European workmen in manufacturing industries, since present industrial conditions do not allow of the constant advance of wages, which there was in the first three quarters of this century, and on the regularity of which workmen had counted. The development of competition has lessened the profits of industries, and for the moment wages also have inevitably been lowered: under these new circumstances it is needful to have recourse to all possible economies, and, above all, to suppress unnecessary expenses. This the

c

workmen in many cities have understood, and the rapid progress of distributing societies in the last few years proves it.

In spite of the general need, the rise of co-operative societies is obstructed by ignorance and that tendency to conservatism which is an enemy to all innovation. Co-operation is the daughter of confidence, ignorance the mother of suspicion; and therefore it is that co-operative societies are seen to spring up with difficulty among country people, often ignorant and distrustful. It is quite true that where simple products in general use are cultivated, the need of these societies is less felt than in cities; but even where, most of all, plantations are cultivated and the labourers receive a wage wholly in money, co-operation has made but little way. Thus if education is desirable for all, it is indispensable for co-operators,[1] and there cannot be swift and constant economic progress, unless it be co-ordinate with intellectual and moral progress.

The tendency to conservatism is a most powerful *vis inertiæ*, and constitutes a serious hindrance to these societies : not even an important advantage can induce consumers to leave off old habits and forsake accustomed shops, and there is still noticed in workmen, and especially in country people,[2] almost everywhere, a sort of apathy as regards these societies.

[1] *Education is life's necessity for co-operators*, Holyoake.
[2] "Our country workman," writes Signor Mantica, (*Relazione sui*

Experience has generally proved that where sound economical doctrines are little diffused, distributing societies can only succeed where a group of individuals previously united by a community of interests and sentiments, furnishes them with a sufficient and secure custom.

If distributing societies succeeded better than any other form of co-operation, because their organisation is very simple, it must not be believed that the office of buying in order to sell retail can always be exercised without risk. A less than microscopic grain of scepticism might often have saved many societies

forni rurali, il pane e la pellegra nel Friuli, Udine, 1888), "does not care to change his habits, nor even to disturb himself in order to go and receive bread in one place rather than another."

The syndics of the distributing co-operative society of Parma, in their report on the 31st December, 1888, wrote, "We cannot but deplore the apathy of members, who have not come up to our expectations, while *less than half* have presented themselves to our sellers for their provisions. It is proper that all should remember that our association is entitled co-operative; and that whoever has given in his adhesion has faced the imprescriptible obligation of keeping it alive."

Many societies in their statute have established a penalty in the case of any who should cease purchasing at the joint-store. The Rochdale Society (art. 5 of the statute) lays down : "No one can continue to be a member who does not purchase from the society to the extent of, at least, four pounds *per annum.*" The Quinzano Society has resolved that the member who does not make purchases at the store for a week shall be expelled. The Magliano decrees expulsion and loss of shares against the member who makes purchases outside the joint-store.

from ruin; co-operation must be practised with sense and prudence, and if men are incapable of giving effect to it, it is not the word "co-operation" which can work miracles.

I firmly believe that no distributing society can succeed without able, active, and honest administrators. Gladstone has declared "wherever good, capable, and trustworthy directors are found, I unreservedly recommend co-operation." For the function of a small dealer there are not needed the valuable qualities of a great merchant, nor intellect, nor special studies, and thus it is not impossible to find persons adapted for this office. In order to avoid risk it is well sometimes to let the sale on lease, and possibly also the management of the store, to a tradesman who gives security and attends to it personally with his family, in return for a percentage on the takings and a maximum being accorded him, regulated by the diminishing of the goods. Generally it is recommended that managers should be well paid and should be interested in the development of the society by means of a remuneration proportionate to the amount of business, or a percentage on the takings over and above a fixed stipend.

There must always be attentive and constant supervision on the part of members, who, as is found in the history of many English co-operative societies, must not disdain, in case of need, to act as assistants for the distribution of goods; and above all it is needful not to be hasty in wishing for splendid results. In Italy, however, there are not wanting too many instances of excellent persons, who, from a momentary enthusiasm for co-operative societies, have preached them up as the best means for putting an end to many social evils, but in practice, astonished at the slowness of their progress, due in a large measure to their having conformed to certain barren principles, speedily lapse from ready enthusiasm into unmanly discouragement and distrust regarding an institution from which they hoped relief for working-men, honour and glory for themselves, in the shape, if so be, of some cross.

But the good choice of managers and the greatest diligence in keeping accounts, which, however, ought to be warmly recommended to co-operative societies, do not yet suffice for the substitution of the society in every branch of retail trade. There is nothing, perhaps, impossible in the moral order, but experience hitherto has shown that distributing societies do not succeed in the case of those services which require special aptitude[1] in the *personnel*, and that they cannot undertake new branches of trade not regularly organised. Initiative is proper for speculation, which

---

[1] Co-operative slaughter-houses have not, as a rule, succeeded in Italy or abroad, possibly owing to the lack of good judges of cattle and the great ease with which one is deceived.

can, and sometimes ought, to be daring; these associations, on the contrary, must never attempt risky enterprises. Distributing societies cannot easily undertake the sale of goods which require great care for their preservation, and easily deteriorate in long warehousing (fresh meat, butter, fresh fruit, etc.); nor of those which require large stores (wood); and generally they must guard against making large purchases wholesale, preferring to make new purchases when the articles in stock diminish.

Thus distributing societies which cannot be substituted in every branch eliminate only the useless traders; and precisely through the co-existence of traders and co-operative societies it will be open to many to convince themselves that it is a blunder to suppose all retail dealers thieves and parasites, and working-men especially will be convinced that it is not manual labour only that is economically productive.

It has been said that the best means of conquering the hindrances referred to, and of making sure progress, is for distributing societies to look up, to have lofty ideals: this is well enough, but in aspiring high it is needful carefully to consider the difficulties of the road and proceed with slow and measured pace, like that of Alpine climbers, with that calm which is imparted by faith in a good idea.

Ought co-operative societies to be limited to some group or class of persons?

There is no reason why these societies founded in the interest of all consumers should restrict their efficacy to some of them, and co-operators, shrinking from close mediæval corporations, refuse every restriction which has no sufficient motives.

There are those who are willing to admit distributing societies only in the case of poor people,[1] workmen, and persons who are badly off. But if poor people have greater need than others to economise, and, thus, to have recourse to the co-operative system, all consumers ought to be able to profit by it. On this point the Court of Cassation at Turin (sentence, 20th July, 1887) observed with fine discretion :—" It is impossible to draw a distinction between people who are well-to-do and those who are not; since

[1] *L'esercente*, a Milan paper, on 19th January, 1890, wrote: "We demand that all persons having rights in the co-operative society should be obliged to present their certificate of misery (!) As such certificates must be given out by the municipal authorities, it will be easy for those to know whether it is advisable to grant them to all who ask for them. Whoever wishes to be treated as a rich man, let him pay what he *ought* to pay ; for, after all, if the tradesman puts ten *lire* into his till for a bottle of champagne, he gives three of them to the Government and the municipality by way of imposts."

But, pray, does paying what one ought mean that traders should grow fat at the expense of honest workmen? Properly, this word can have no other meaning, for co-operative institutions are not benefit societies, nor can he, the writer of the article cited, allude to fiscal privileges which Italian co-operative societies certainly do not enjoy.

reason, good sense, and the smallest experience of life show how difficult, risky, and treacherous this undertaking is, and into what irreparable mistakes a sentence may be drawn which should be pronounced with such a calculation. The humble labourer who pushes railway carriages on the line for wages of two *lire* a day, may sometimes have fewer needs and be better off relatively to his position than the official of rank and respectability, engaged in the same administration at three thousand francs or more *per annum*. This is a truth which does not need demonstrating, since it is evident at a glance."

The democratic spirit which breathes in every modern institution, cannot be wanting in distributing societies, and should prevent a privilege being formed by them in the interests of *anybody*. It is well that the richer classes, placed in better circumstances, through wealth and education, should share also in the co-operative societies of working-men, because, especially in small towns, the well-to-do can spend several hours a day in the administration of the society without serious loss; whereas, the working-man, who has small knowledge of business and little time, can with difficulty do so. If co-operative societies ought to refuse all material support, they ought not to scorn this spontaneous and not humiliating intervention of the well-to-do, who aim at combining the interests of the society with their own—that of saving on consumption.

Among us many societies still rigorously limit the right of membership to certain groups[1] of persons.

One motive for exclusion is sometimes found in the importance assigned to personal dignity; thus many societies only receive officials as members. Co-operative societies among railway officials, which are some of the most powerful and best known among us, have a special motive for excluding other persons, since the railway companies grant special and important benefits on the very just condition that they are applied exclusively in the interest of their respective *personnel*. This rigorous limitation to a group of persons is only possible where the class of persons constituting the society is very numerous; hence these societies are prosperous only in large centres of population.

Politics, also, are sometimes a cause of exclusion; a

---

[1] The Working-men's Distributing Society at Schio requires that the members should be working-men or live on the wages of manual labour. Thus, the rules of the Ardazeno Society declare that those only can be effective members who live by the daily product of their labour. In the Collegno Store only the workmen of the Gattoni Mill are received, it being provided in the rules that if a member ceases to be attached to the mill, he can no longer form part of the society. The Migliano Co-operative Society only accepts as members the working-men of the Noma Cotton-mill. That of Biandrate, in an article on the subject, lays it down that only country-people and working-men may belong to the society.

society founded by clericals does not accept freemasons, nor does one established by socialists consent to admit conservatives. But it is well that politics, with its passions, should not be mixed up with co-operation any more than with social questions generally; in this respect Italian co-operators are worthy of high praise, who, although belonging to opposite political parties, are able, with fine practical sense, to unite and work together for co-operative ideals.

Furthermore, there is no need to exclude women from distributing societies, which directly affect their sphere of action, since they are specially concerned with domestic economy. The hostility of the women has often impeded the development of these societies; a woman must make great efforts before she can accustom herself to ready-money payment; and the working-man's wife will prefer, for instance, to obtain a reduction after haggling about the price than buy cheap at fixed prices, a natural condition for all co-operative societies. While the woman who is hostile to co-operative societies can injure it in a thousand ways, by declaring that the commodities are not good, or too dear, and dissuading her husband from taking part in the meetings, where he loses precious time in thankless labours; the woman who is favourable to it, is the best instrument of propaganda, and by her purchases at the stores, and her practical and sagacious counsels, becomes a most useful element in co-operative societies.

CHAPTER IV.

DIFFERENT FORMS OF DISTRIBUTING CO-OPERATIVE SOCIETIES.

SCHÖNBERG[1] classifies distributing societies according to the nature of the goods which they distribute: thus there are societies for firing, societies for eatables, for clothes, for lighting, etc. This distinction does not seem to be acceptable, since it is based on an extrinsic element which seldom exactly corresponds with the real state of affairs; whilst in Germany, owing to the unlimited responsibility of members, which largely restricts the number of goods so as to do away with risks of loss, and owing to the special economical conditions of the German working-classes, very few societies sell many objects, and thus Schönberg's division is almost always practicable, in England and other countries, where distributing societies sell every sort of goods, it is impossible.

Our own division is a most important one—that of provident stores or committees and distributing socie-

[1] *Die Landwirthschaft der Gegenwart und die Genossenschaft s princip.* Berlin, 1869.

ties properly so-called. The first, widely diffused among us, having almost invariably arisen through the initiative of mutual aid-societies, sell at the lowest prices, not always for cash payment, and exclusively to members: the others, on the contrary, conform to the English or Rochdalian system, as it is called, that of selling at the current market prices, never on trust, to members and non-members, and with a participation in the profits by non-members.

With these differences I fully deal later on, since on account of their importance they deserve special treatment.

There is, moreover, universally received another distinction between societies which sell on their own account and those which agree with the traders of the place, who, in order to secure constant and abundant custom, and from the certainty of payment, grant a fixed reduction to members, determined at so much per cent. on the normal price of the goods.

The method of working these societies, which had a wide development in Germany, is very simple. The society sells to its members counters or tokens (whence the name *marken-system* for this form of distributing society) for their nominal value, and with these members make purchases in the shops agreeing with the society: the society, at certain stated intervals, generally once a week, takes back the counters from the several purveyors, and, with the deductions stipulated, changes them into money and retains the compensation per cent. before fixed upon, which is exactly the advantage accruing to the society. The counters must be of different sorts; since in the agreements with a number of purveyors, different reductions have been stipulated; otherwise it would be only too easy for a tradesman who had granted a large reduction to get his counters presented by another who granted a smaller reduction. The society, after subtracting the expenses, makes a calculation, in the distribution of profits among the consumers, of the different kinds of counters used by each member in order to get at the precise amount of the purchases made by the members.

Some societies use, instead of counters, receipts: then the member pays the purveyor in ready money and at current prices, and the latter hands him a receipt. On the total of these receipts the society afterwards exacts the reduction agreed upon. By this method the society saves the expense of the counters and their distribution, runs none of the risks inherent in having large sums in cash, and the purveyor can grant a larger reduction, since he is not obliged to give credit to the society up to the time of the tokens being changed for money. This system, however, is objectionable, because, usually, in order to avoid the trouble of making out as many receipts as there are purchases, purveyors grant the stipulated reduction on the price to the members direct, and thus the society is gradually rendered useless.

Whether it is preferable to start a direct sale, or to arrange leases with different purveyors, depends on the circumstances of each society, which it is always necessary to take into account. Certainly, by carrying on a sale of its own, by conducting an enterprise at the common risk, if things turn out well and capital is not defective, benefits can be obtained far superior to the reduction which can be granted by tradesmen.

It has been observed, too, that it is more advantageous, in small towns, to have a sale proper than to make contracts, because, where the inhabitants know each other, it is easier to find a good manager, because the renting of premises costs less, and because the competition between traders being very small, they are with difficulty induced to make contracts for supplying at reduced prices; it is observed, however, as a set off, that in small centres it is difficult to put together the necessary capital in order to form a joint store.

The system of leases is not without advantages: it saves the expense of a store and sale, it does away with the danger of being deceived in the purchases, and obviates the very serious difficulty of finding able managers. But it yields smaller advantages and makes it difficult to observe whether the purveyors do not indemnify themselves for the reduction covenanted on the weight or in the measure, or by altering the prices of the goods. In order to prevent an alteration of the prices, which would make the reduction fictitious, it will be well to arrange leases only with those tradesmen who sell at fixed prices. In spite, however, of possible deceptions, there is always the advantage of enticing consumers, especially workingmen, who are for the most part improvident, to make imperceptibly small savings consisting in real or fictitious discounts, which are given back at the end of the year.

The societies which adopt the system of leases cannot be termed, with precision, distributing co-operative societies, since in reality they do not fulfil the office of purchasing in order to distribute to members; and they are to be considered rather as an embryo of distributing societies, which may be gradually developed when a sufficient capital has been formed and the number of members has been collected necessary for starting a sale. An interesting type of these societies is that of the food supplies of A. Grandi, founded in 1880 at Rome. He made an agreement with different provision dealers, scattered all over Rome, who grant a reduction of 5 per cent. on the purchases made by workmen attached to the supplies: this saving is capitalised in the interest of the purchaser, and when it has attained the sum twenty *lire*, these are converted into a share in the " food supplies," where goods are purchased at reduced prices. It is an ingenious way of getting together a capital; it is, as Luzzati says, a sound and simple idea, not free from defects, but one by which all may profit, which costs nothing, and which may produce incalculable benefits.

Many distributing societies, besides keeping a store for some goods, make contracts with purveyors for others, in order to enjoy the advantages of both systems. This is done, for instance, by the co-operative society of Geneva which, although it has been in existence for 23 years and has six shops, nevertheless has not believed itself able to undertake the sale of meat, bread, and certain other commodities, and for these articles makes provision contracts with tradesmen, who sell their goods, at an important reduction, to its members.

It is the custom with us also, in the interest of members of real co-operative societies, to obtain reductions from retail dealers on the prices of goods which are not distributed by the society. Generally, however, the reductions are granted from time to time on each single purchase, whereas it would be much more serviceable to get in the economies, which have been obtained through profiting by the facilities granted to the society, at the end of the year. I think it expedient, in this chapter, to speak of rural co-operative bake-houses, a form of distributing society which, owing to special traits which it has acquired in Italy, departs, in a large measure, from pure co-operative principles.

Rural bake-houses, which were tried in Lombardy as far back as 1860—the first appears to have been instituted at Corte Palasio (Lodi) by an engineer, A. Reschisi—began to be known in 1878 through the zealous propagandism of a clergyman, Don R. Anelli, who had already won the prize offered by the Agricultural Society of Lombardy by his essay, *Miglioramento del pane del contadino*, and through whose means there arose, a few at a time, more than eighty rural bake-houses.

These bake-houses are widely diffused abroad also. At Baden and at Würtemberg there are economic bake-houses which the rural municipalities now look upon as an indispensable institution; there are also a large number in Scotland and France.

Since the chief object of these bake-houses still is to improve the quality of the countryman's bread, private individuals and Government have made it their business to favour the institution of them, and by the introduction of patronage have disturbed the pure co-operative element. The hygienic importance of these bake-houses is truly very great, since they remove many causes of pellagra[1] by avoiding the

[1] *Penicellum glaucum*, a fungus which is developed during the fermentation of corn kept in a damp place, is, according to Lombroso, the direct cause of pellagra.

incomplete drying and storing of grain in ill-ventilated places, the making of loaves of excessive dimensions, badly baked, and containing little salt. Fresh bread, well-baked and well made, is a real windfall for our country people, who are seven or eight days, and, in the winter, even fifteen fashioning a loaf, which, after five days, turns sour through excessive dampness due to the insufficient heating of the oven, to the incomplete duration of the baking, and which cannot be wholesome and sufficient nourishment for the country people.

The Government, considering the important advantages of these bake-houses and the serious difficulty of collecting the amount required for the plant, resolved, by a decree of 23rd March, 1884, to contribute half the cost of the plant of the new bake-houses which were being established. In consequence of this decree many bake-houses, called co-operative, are frequently benefit institutions. Signor Mantica, in his report on the bake-houses of Friuli, already quoted, writes that there, with the exception of that at Felotto, the bake-houses have nothing social or co-operative about them; and, in truth, the promoters reckoned exclusively for the plant on the assistance of the municipality, the Province, or the Government, and introduced the words co-operation, shareholders, councillors, etc., for the sole object of rendering possible the subsidies granted by the Minister of Agriculture, by the decree of 1884, to those bake-houses established without any speculative aim, with a preference for those having a co-operative aim.

An instance of a bake-house which is called co-operative, but in reality is not, is the rural bake-house of Villanterio (Pavia), established with a capital of 3,500 *lire* collected on the pretext of benevolence, and which permanently enjoys the grant of premises, made to it by the municipality, for the store. The bake-house has no members, and its office is to buy in order to sell retail without speculation; now the bake-house has very many customers, and sells at current prices or returns bread to any one who delivers wheat to it in the proportion of 124 kilograms of bread for 100 of wheat. The manager has absolutely a free hand in the selection of the raw materials, and in fixing the price of the product; and this is the principal cause of the prosperity of this bake-house, while the absence of this condition was often the reason of co-operative bake-houses failing. Naturally great praise is due to the manager, Signor Gulielmini, who has succeeded, by his zeal and ability, in giving such an extension to the bake-house as to collect about four thousand *lire* as a reserve, which, it is to be hoped, may so far increase as to allow of a mill being set up; and the council of administration, including the parson and the doctor retained, are to be praised also for their constant supervision of the enterprise.

Before finishing this chapter it will be as well to make mention of another form of distributing society —food societies or co-operative restaurants,[1] because certain inconveniences discovered in them have a tendency to extend to all distributing societies. In spending in public, before the eyes of acquaintances and strangers, all intention, it is said, of saving vanishes. Through an ill-understood self-love, people do not wish to seem inferior to their neighbours, and rather than abet the honourable motives of some self-denial, renounce them, and spend, moreover, beyond their own means and necessities. Again, it is said that going to a restaurant makes the needs of a home less felt, and loosens the ties of family already too much relaxed.

---

[1] These societies must not be confounded with economic kitchens for the benefit of the poor, very widely diffused in Italy and abroad. In Switzerland (Geneva) and in Germany (Berlin, Breslau, Hamburg, etc.) there are *Volkskaffechaüser*, generally opened through the agency of Temperance Societies, where there is a cup of coffee or thick soup for five *pfennige*, and for ten *pfennige* a cup of tea or a glass of beer or two sausages. In England, in the penny dinners, for ten *centesimi*, you may breakfast on cold milk, bread and butter. In Catalonia the numerous *restaurans de obreras* are also, as Bernabi observes, benefit institutions, "*per quantos los alimentos que preparan se venden a un precio inferior al de su coste, supliendo el deficit con los donativos y recursos que la caridad suministra.*

But in these considerations also we must carefully guard against exaggerating. If an unmarried official, who does not dine at home, succeeds in coming to an agreement with other colleagues, and they set up a co-operative restaurant on their joint account, is it absolutely necessary that he should become a drunkard simply through having his belly full of good food or saving on the fare? Thus, for example, in the case of many workmen in great factories, who, in order to avoid trouble and loss of time, are compelled to bring their food with them and always to eat it cold, except for drinking a small glass of brandy as the single article of diet which possesses an apparent calorific power, would not a co-operative kitchen, where drinks and hot food might be purchased with an important saving, be of great utility, and would it not contribute also to lessen the evils of drunkenness, which, whether the cause or effect of misery, is a potent source of mischief?

It has been said that the nations which progress most rapidly are those which eat the most: and when an institution, besides procuring better fare, offers an important economy of time and money (shown by the purchase wholesale and at first hand of articles prepared by a small number of persons for hundreds of consumers, and for a smaller waste of fuel than there is cooking separately, a saving still more felt when the kitchen works by steam), and, what is more, with the habit of saving brings a moral progress, who will reject it, and, on account of certain doubtful moral defects, refuse the important advantages which it secures on given conditions and for determinate classes of persons?

CHAPTER V.

SOME QUESTIONS RELATIVE TO THE CARRYING ON OF DISTRIBUTING CO-OPERATIVE SOCIETIES.

(a) Whether one ought to sell on credit.

THERE is no greater danger for co-operative societies than the practice of selling on credit.

By ready-money payment distributing societies have the great advantage of not incurring losses through bad debts, of having a simple system of accounts, a less complicated administration, of not involving the society in the costs of legal disputes, and of shutting the door on remonstrances in case the credit be denied, qualified or disowned. Further, by cash payment the society has no need to buy wholesale on credit, and is thus certain to obtain the lowest possible prices, and may, with very little capital, have a large circle of business, while its operations are always safe.

In the provision system *(Markensystem)* the society which sold its tokens on credit would find itself incommoded in paying the purveyors, which would lead to the reduction granted by them being diminished.

While the consumer finds it very advantageous to buy on credit, the private tradesman willingly sells on credit at a short term of payment, in order to hold the debtor bound, and to assure himself of a certain custom. Thus the debtor is not absolutely free ("he who is in debt is owned by others"), and he often finds in the credit which attracts him, and which favours and encourages improvidence, his own ruin.

The tradesman, in order to protect himself from every risk proceeding from credit, is accustomed to raise the price of the goods, and this rise has been estimated at twenty per cent. of the price : thus even those consumers who pay ready money must pay something in addition for the benefit of bad payers, and a privilege, as it were, is formed for the benefit of these last which the trader sometimes avoids by conceding a special reduction to any one paying ready-money.[1]

---

[1] To show the importance of this fact I may mention that in Germany was conceived a large general institute for economy and rebate (*Rabbat-Spar-Anstalt*) in the purchase of all kind of things. To this institute were to belong, as members, as well those traders who sell the articles as those who buy them. The mechanism was to be as follows : To any one paying immediately a reduction is conceded represented by a check which is delivered by the seller. The buyer makes a collection of these

In theory, for the reasons which have been briefly pointed out, almost all co-operators are agreed in preferring ready-money sale, but in practice there are too many exceptions to the theory, and it will seem strange that in England itself, the classic land of distributing societies, where the command of never forsaking the principle of buying and selling for ready-money, dictated at Rochdale, ought to prevail, the system of selling on credit is relatively much diffused.

A recent work by Mr. J. C. Gray [1] deals with the

checks for very small sums and demands payment when they have reached a given cipher. The vendor pays into the institute the small fractions for which he has issued checks, and these are forthwith laid out for the benefit of buyers. There would thus be the gain of avoiding many of those purchases on credit so adverse to domestic economy, and a person, after buying and paying immediately for several things, would find that he had effected, without being aware of it, a small saving. The thing would be profitable also to vendors, who would be sure of being paid. Kuntze, in his proposal, has thought of adopting, instead of the checks referred to, savings-tokens. Any one buying to the amount of a *mark* would have a five *pfennige* one, and these tokens would serve to constitute a closed savings bank memorandum book. (A. Codacci-Pisanelli, *L'Ordinamento delle Casse di Risparmio in Germania*, Rome, 1885 p. 146.) Evidently the advantages which this institution presents are inferior to those of distributing co-operative societies which permit of a larger reduction, guarantee the quality and quantity of the goods, and act, within certain limits, as savings banks.

[1] *The System of Credit as practised by Co-operative Societies*, published in the Co-operative Wholesale Societies' Annual for 1889, Manchester, 1889.

perilous spread ("alarming extent") of sale on credit. From this it appears that in 1886, of 1228 societies selling retail, which had forwarded their balance sheets to the central office, 698, of which 488 were English, 15 Welsh, 190 Scotch and 5 Irish, sold on credit. The system was carried out by different methods, which Gray, giving the precedence to the most harmful, thus graduates :—

1. Without limitations or conditions: of these societies 69 are English, 2 Welsh and 6 Scotch.

2. Limited by a term of payment: of these societies 113 are English, 9 Scotch, 1 Irish, and 2 Welsh.

3. Limited to a certain determinate sum in the cases of each member: in this category are 77 English societies, 2 Welsh, and 6 Scotch.

4. Limited to a certain amount proportioned to each member's capital in shares : this category is made up of 168 English, 155 Scotch and 4 Irish.

5. Restricted to special goods, such as coal, bread, flour, stuffs, with limitations also in the time of payment.

The societies belonging to the first three classes are on a road which is absolutely dangerous ; those of the others only restrain an evil which ought to be altogether avoided. The fact is, if one prospered in spite of credit, others were ruined on account of credit, and it is certain that constant draughts on the capital caused many societies to lose strength and elasticity in business. One fault of these societies, more evident in those of the fourth category, is to consider the share capital as a banking deposit, while its exclusive use to the society ought to be, to render the market accessible, and enable it to buy on the most advantageous terms.

The pretexts adopted by co-operative societies in order to excuse the introduction of credit are of various kinds, but they may be reduced to these: wages paid at too long intervals, especially in the case of country people and miners, sickness, want of work, misery, living at a distance from the joint store, which necessitates children being sent on errands, who must not be trusted with money, or requires the purchase of provisions on a large scale and only on given days; lastly, the prevailing excuse, the customs of the place and the need of competing with retail traders.

To the first pretext, not a new one, Garelli[1] in 1874 replied thus: " Vice has always an excuse at hand, and those who do not pay, advance theirs likewise. They say that it is a necessity, as their wages are not sufficient for their needs. But it is false, and the fact proves it. They buy for a month on credit, and then pay. The next month they again ask for a respite, and so continually; the result is that they pay in the end, but always a month too late. Let them gain this month, and they will find themselves straight. Does

[1] *I salari e la classe operaia in Italia*, Torino, 1871.

it require such an effort on the part of those to whom it *is* an effort to arrive at this ? The first co-operative societies which took up this position had a good deal to contend with, but they stood firm, and it is to that they must attribute, in a particular way, their splendid results."

The excuse of having to send children is certainly not very serious, since as a rule, if they are capable of buying goods, they will be able also to carry money to the store. A still less serious excuse is the wish to follow the custom of the locality so as to compete with small traders: co-operative societies should be able to introduce improvements into trading customs and domestic economy, and therefore should not make the ruinous path of debt easy to consumers.

On the other hand, the question is worthy of consideration, whether it is not injustice to refuse purchase on credit to a steady and hard-working member who, through illness or some other cause not attributable to him, cannot pay. In these cases it would be better, instead of selling on credit, to give councils of administration the power to grant loans, which would only be made to deserving persons, on security, and for a definite object. These cases, however, will be rare with those societies which sell at market prices, and teach people to hoard their savings, to which the member will be able to have recourse in case of need.

Thus it is never necessary to depart from the

ready-money sale, the opposite system being a real misfortune for co-operative societies. It is impossible to calculate precisely the losses sustained by English societies through credit; anyway 195 societies admit having had losses, and it has been proved that the decline of many societies, even of those which at first promised well, was occasioned by sale on credit.

In Germany also they sometimes sell on credit, and according to a calculation of Schneider,[1] the societies which sell on credit are more than 25 per cent.; the practice most commonly is to give credit for firing and potatoes, in order to enable members to lay in a sufficient stock for the winter. Some years ago, in condemning sale on credit, Schulze-Delitzsch repeatedly advised distributing co-operative societies to accustom the people to immediate payment for the goods purchased, and attributed the ruin of many of them, before anything else, to their abuse of credit.

In Italy also not a few co-operative societies sell on credit, though almost always with some restriction.[2]

---

[1] *Co-operative News*, 6th July, 1889.

[2] At Treviso credit is granted to the extent of the sums paid in advance: at Murano and S. Maria Capua Vetere up to three-quarters of the shares held: at Lari to the extent of 50 *lire*: at Magliano and Collegno to the amount of the sums invested, but in case of illness up to two-thirds of the shares paid up. At Livorno credit is limited to 40 *lire* for the first share

One obstacle to the development of co-operative societies is sale on credit among traders, which keeps the debtor bound to the retail dealer, and prevents the former from making purchases and joining a co-operative society. In order to assist him to free himself from debt, many societies in England employ the reserve fund in making advances to workmen, who would like to become members, but are prevented by debts contracted with retail dealers: with these advances, obtained on the personal security of those who possess in the society a sum equal or superior to that which is advanced, they pay their creditors, gradually reimbursing the society by the dividends of the profits on the purchases.

A co-operative store, besides not granting credit, does all in its power to assist members not to have

subscribed, and 20 *lire* in excess of the said 40 *lire* for each of the remaining shares subscribed, but altogether the credit may not exceed 200 *lire:* at Foligno credit is allowed up to three-quarters of the month's wages : at Florence credit is limited to a sum equivalent to the shares paid : at Pisa credit is open to all the shareholders, even if the amount of the shares has not been fully paid, but within three days from payment it is necessary to extinguish the debts, and a respite is granted only in case of illness. There is sale on credit also at Casciarola, Sesto Fiorentino, Bologna, etc. All railway co-operative societies sell on credit, but at the end of a month they have a right to draw on the wages of tardy members. The military union sells on credit to mounted officers being shareholders up to 400 *lire* ; to non-members, mounted, up to 300 *lire*, binding, however, officers who avail themselves of credit to various monthly gages.

need of it. Thus the Borgo Lavezzaro store, whose members are nearly all country people, permits them to deposit in the society's chest a weekly quota, intended to form a personal credit. The depositing may take place from March to November, and must not exceed 100 *lire* a year; every member who is a creditor of the society will be able to draw goods during the three months December, January, and February, when country people have frequently no work, until his saving is extinguished; but, with rare exceptions, drawing sums of money is not allowed.

Veron expounds with enthusiasm a simple method for preventing the workman feeling too often the need of having recourse to credit. The society offers to exchange the money which the workman receives at the end of the week for tokens which are afterwards received by the society as current coin. Here is coin writes Veron, which can be guarded without disquietude, and which will not tempt the workman, because it has no currency in public-houses. Thus the association, besides being an economic and hygienic institution, is also a provident institution.

Distributing societies must seek in every way to diffuse the practice of buying ready-money, and must carefully remember that "credit to consumption is credit to indolence, and if there is a true desire for the economic and social improvement of the working-classes, it is necessary to wean them from buying on credit."

(b) *Whether the distribution of goods ought to be made at the lowest prices, or at the current market prices.*

Co-operative societies sell either at cost price, augmented by the expense of the joint administration, or at a higher price, permitting the accumulation of capital.

It is not a matter of indifference whether the one or the other system be adopted: with the sale at cost price, practised by provident committees, the member's gain is reduced to an increase in his consumption, and thus day by day insensibly evaporates; with the sale at the current market-prices, and the distribution of savings at certain periods (quarter, half-year, year), the small savings obtained from time to time are treasured up, and by the formation of a capital there is rendered possible a social evolution, by means of which poverty will gradually be able to attain comfort.

But at once, before the advantages of the one or other system of sale are considered, the objection is presented that sale at current prices is unjust and should not even be discussed, because it favours the formation of a capital. On this principle a co-operative programme was formulated thus:[1] "Organisation of the means of transforming and distributing food by means of associations which have no object of gain or saving, but simply and only that of giving back to the labourers the entire fruit of their labour by removing all parasitical organs which are the cause of the present ills."

It is not possible for me to show how unjust is this blind hatred of capital by which many socialists are possessed; but leaving on one side abstract questions of justice, and attending only to the actual economic conditions, since it is a fact that the possession of capital secures advantages, why should not one facilitate the enjoyment of these advantages by the needy classes and oppose to the immoderate accumulation of money by a few a more even distribution of wealth for the relief of consumers, even the poorest? The programme cited appears to be inspired by the cry of French socialist workmen, "*l'ouvrier qui épargne est un traître*," entirely forgetting that the object of distributing associations is exactly that of saving—whether or not they accumulate these savings—for the benefit of consumers. It is, therefore, a curious programme which desires institutions for saving whilst it does not desire saving itself.

Without the formation of a capital, the true im-

[1] Dr. G. Maffei and P. Artioli, *Organizzazione nazionale della cooperazione di consumo*, Reggio Emilia, 1886.

portance of distributing co-operative societies would cease.

It has been calculated—a very elastic calculation, of course—that a family of working-people purchasing all the objects which it needs from distributing societies, can save from 50 to 60 *centesimi* a day. Now, who will doubt but that it will be far more profitable to this family to receive at the end of the year from 180 to 200 *lire*, which may serve, for instance, to pay the rent of the house, instead of daily enjoying a saving which can with difficulty be accumulated? The increase in consumption, the principal advantage of sale at cost price, is not always advantageous: if the workman spends the fifty *centesimi*, saved by means of distributing societies, in wine or liquors at the public-house, all possibility of the workman's improvement vanishes. Nor can the wish of Henry IV., that the poor should have a chicken every feast-day, be the ideal of distributing societies: after a hundred years the poor will ever remain such with sale at the lowest prices.

Who will not prefer a system which procures for every family of working-people, without any sacrifice on their part, a sum, relatively so important, which serves powerfully to lessen that misery which the labouring classes sometimes cry out upon as unjust and threaten with violence to stop, which brings love and respect for capital, and which in increased economic welfare ensures a moral and intellectual progress? It is by the formation of a capital that the high aims of co-operation can be attained and give rise to manufacturing co-operative societies, by which many persons trust to put an end to all economic trouble.

Nor is it impossible that this ideal of distributing societies should be attained in Italy and abroad: the example of saving must come from educated persons, and the useful initiative taken by the English democracy shows that the indifference and ignorance of the poor are not insuperable obstacles to sale at prices current. And I maintain as indisputable that if all courtiers of the people, instead of glorifying the working-men, the most flattered class of all, exciting, as they may, social disturbances, had always actively and consistently favoured and promoted institutions like these, there would have been fewer evils to lament, and the ideal of co-operators would not have been called, as they are now, "dreams of astrologers and alchemists."

There is no doubt that workmen, not sufficiently educated and instructed, prefer, as the proverb says, "an egg to-day to a hen to-morrow," and aim at immediate advantages. On this subject I record Mac-Culloch's observation.[1] "Poverty, like vice, is never so little dreaded as by those who find themselves immersed in it. It is a common remark that the lower

---

[1] *Elementi che determinano la meta delle mercedi*, capo iv. Bibl. dell' Econ., 2ª Serie, vol. iii. trattati speciali.

we descend in the social scale, the nearer we approach the seat of vice and misery; the more are idleness and vice at once the most efficacious cause and most common effect of the misery so much and so justly deplored. Self-control is usually least practised by those to whom it is most profitable. An ignorant and poor population shows itself, like the lowest animals, eager for immediate pleasures. And in order that they may begin to calculate the remote effects of their actions, it is necessary that something should supervene to improve their condition, making them to feel the folly and baseness of their former conduct." Distributing societies, with sale at current prices, show the rage for immediate pleasures to be folly, and accustom people to a saving which is very difficult to be begun and practised by any one earning little more than is necessary in order to live.

By MacCulloch's observation is explained the very rapid development of societies which sell at the lowest prices, and the slow development of the others; while, however, the first, even the best administered, become almost stationary, the others continue steadily to progress.

With the sale at cost price the member is attracted to the society only by the greater advantages which it offers him in comparison with other shops, and he profits by it as he might by any shop which should grant large reductions in order to have many customers; he runs to it with great readiness, and the members soon become very numerous. When, on the other hand, the savings are collected by the society and are afterwards distributed to each member, the advantage is not immediate, and the growth of the society is impeded by the ignorance and improvidence of those who cannot wait for accounts to be made up and have no reliance on an unknown principle. But if the balance-sheet is favourable and the member can see the amount of his savings and hold in his hand, for instance, a bill for twenty *lire* at the end of the year, he finds himself much better pleased than if he had had a few *centesimi* every time, spreads abroad these advantages, and the progress of the society is guaranteed.

While the members of a store which sells at the lowest prices express regret, often with strange insistence, in regard to those articles which do not give an important saving in comparison with other shops, because tradesmen renounce almost all gain on them, such as sugar, petroleum, etc., and as though not knowing the advantages of them, are silent as to the other articles; complaints are hardly ever heard where the daily economies are accumulated and divided every year, because the members know that the results are obtained from the balance-sheet. Inasmuch as the member must look for the profits of the business from the balance-sheet, he has an interest in the payment of them being guaranteed to him by a good administration. Besides making a good choice of administrators, the member is interested in their not slackening their activity and zeal, in order that the dividend, the surest measure of the work of administration, may not be lessened; and therefore he constantly watches over the general interests. The administrators, on the other hand, cannot conceal a diminution of the dividend arising from a bad management of the undertaking, since they cannot raise the price of goods beyond what is current without finding themselves deserted by purchasers, and they are therefore stimulated to redouble their efforts that a want of confidence may not be felt in them: in other words, the administrators occupy a difficult position in the face of the members, and for that reason they will be more zealous and diligent in maintaining it.

With sale at the lowest possible prices it is of no immediate economic interest to any one that a balance should be struck, and no one has any special motives for looking after the administrators. With this system, therefore, it is easy to hide a bad administration; if, for instance, in the case of every commodity, the society added to the cost-price a surcharge of 5 per cent. for working expenses, while the tradesmen put 10 per cent. on the commodities, it will not be difficult to charge them with 7 per cent., selling always at a less price than the trader, and remedying the scant ability and honesty of the administrators by an additional 2 per cent. paid on each commodity. The long term of working assists this easy operation.

It happens not unfrequently, when goods are sold at cost price, that the year's working closes with a deficit. In point of fact all the expenses cannot be calculated from the beginning, and some may well escape notice when the percentage is being settled with which to charge commodities in order to meet the general expenses. And if it happened that the price of a given commodity, sold by the society at cost price, should be so reduced in the market that business men were able to sell it at a less price than the society, the latter would find itself exposed to serious loss, which could not always be concealed.[1]

---

[1] This consideration has engaged the attention of the members of the Mezzana-Montaldo Society, who, in order to protect themselves from eventual losses, have thus resolved in their statute : "Since it comes to pass that while goods, purchased in large quantities for a definite amount, are being consumed, their price diminishes in general trade, the administration Council shall have a right to fix a *minimum* for each member within the peremptory term which shall be appointed, at the average price paid at the time of the purchase. It will fix the *maximum* of purchase for each member when goods rise." This identical arrangement is reproduced in the statutes of the two societies of Mosso S. Maria and Trivero Vandano. Thus with sale at the lowest prices freedom is fettered in the purchases, and consumers are subjected to the indiscreet control of the administrators.

For another reason also sale at current prices assures the progress of co-operative societies. While the society which sells at current prices does not excite serious alarm in traders by whom it is often laughed at as a useless experiment, so long as they perceive no diminution in their customers by reason of the society, one which sells at the lowest possible prices, renders competition very keen for other traders, who, by selling on credit, by making presents at the end of the year, by renouncing all gain on certain goods, by their better acquaintance with wholesale traders and manufacturers, and, generally, by their larger experience of trade, can, even without having recourse to dishonest means, wage a destructive war on distributing societies.[1] When the society which sells at current prices has been established on solid foundations, and traders begin to perceive the loss which accrues to them from it, it, in its turn, will be able to laugh at the slow perception of the traders and their would-be competition.

Another observation is made in support of sale at

[1] At Paris, writes Hubert Valleroux, tradesmen sell sugar almost at cost price, gaining on the weight and quality.

At Lima (United States), writes Warner, the dealers determined with one consent to sell below cost price, some one article, some another, in order to ruin the co-operative store which had sprung up there, and they succeeded. This struggle was very keen, because, as at Thillsboro', in Ohio, the societies ha' announced a wish to destroy all middlemen.

current prices, on the hypothesis, that labour remaining organised as at present, this form of association becomes general.

It is a canon of socialistic teaching, propagated especially by Lassalle, that by means of wages capitalists fleece working-men, the true producers, since the latter are constrained by hunger to accept any agreement. Now, it is said, it is evident that if distributing societies reduce, for instance, the cost of living twenty per cent., wages which are fixed at the minimum necessary for existence will be lowered in proportion.[1] I will not stay here to show that the normal must not be confounded with the necessary wage, and that there is a large element of exaggeration in the principle alluded to; I will merely observe that this danger ceases with sale at currrent prices, which, in this respect, does not alter the conditions of life of

---

[1] Malthus, in his *Essay on the Principle of Population*, quoted by Zorli (*Emancipazione economica della classe operaia*, Bologna, 1881, p. 79), writes:—"I will not stay to discuss the proposals made by various persons, where the question is treated of supplying food at a low price and establishing parish stores and workshops. The good effects of such institutions entirely result from this, that they are peculiar and reserved to certain families and parishes. As soon as it is desired to render all the good effects universal, they disappear, because they tend to lessen wages."

For this very reason Morgan, in a speech made at Chicago, at a meeting of the *International Working People's Association* in November, 1886, warmly opposed distributing societies.

the wage-earners, since the wages are spent in the same proportion as at other traders.

Some observations advanced against sale at current prices are practical exceptions rather than real objections.

Sale at market prices, it is said, is not consonant with equity. Here is an instance of it. The price of quinine in the country districts of Novara was, in 1886, 1·20 *lire* the gram; the Federation of Novara, a distributing society which sells at the lowest prices, now distributes it for only 20 *centesimi* the gram, and it is asked: Would it not be cruel injustice to refuse this immediate boon to the wretched country-people of Novara, where through the miasmas of the rice-fields they are plagued with fevers?

This objection only shows that sale at current prices cannot be applied blindly and everywhere. Thus, when the market-price represents the will imposed by certain dealers, the English system, which may favour an illegitimate raising of prices, must not be applied. So, also, in extraordinary cases of epidemics, dearths, economic and labour crises, it may be expedient to sell at prices lower than those current; but these cases are exceptions, and, in regard to them, the General Assembly will be able advantageously to depart from the English principle. One would need to be a doctrinaire co-operator, or, as the French say, a *coopérateur en chambre* labouring under a great delusion to deny the worth of these exceptions, and not to commend the project of Signor Ponti, which sanctions them (art. 17 and 18). A few exceptions, however, ought not to form the rule.

Another exception has been suggested by Signor Labadini[1] in the case of rural co-operative bake-houses, since the farmer who brings maize or flour to the bake-house that it may be converted into bread, knows, that from a given amount of corn he receives a larger quantity of bread than the baker of the village is accustomed to give his customers who pay ready-money or in grain; whence the co-operative bake-house, which eliminates a few intermediaries, cannot claim that the member should receive a smaller quantity of bread than usual without the association being deserted. For country-people who have a large part of their gains in kind, the services of grinding and making into bread are a subject of compensation, not in money, but in kind. In order to refund to the miller the cost of grinding, the countryman gives grain, not money; in order to refund to the baker the cost of bread-making, he does the same; and when a computation comes to be made of the quantity of bread which shall correspond to the grain or flour delivered, the barter criterion prevails over that of the buying-and-selling contract which would be im-

[1] *Il forno rurale cooperativo*, Roma, 1889, p. 48.

plied in it; and there is a tariff of exchange which, with its alterations, ought to follow all the oscillations of the market-price, but which, on the contrary, tends to become as stable as possible. This, for the speculator, becomes the occasion of frequent and magnificent gains, but, on the contrary, may drag the co-operative concern more quickly to ruin, for the simple reason, that only through reserves of gains is it possible to make head against losses; and the co-operator must avoid the latter without availing himself of the former. But the bake-house must not remain, as Labadini appears to wish, simply an agency for barter, unless it is to abjure all the progress which is represented by commerce and industry[1]; and when there is a real buying-and-selling contract, since the quantity of bread which the grain can yield to the member who should manufacture it privately is less than that obtained by means of a co-operative bake-house,[2] there is no special reason why the saving given by the bake-house, not selling at the lowest prices, should not be accumulated. This system has

[1] Enea Cavalieri, *Il forno rurale cooperativo* in *Credito e co-operazione*, 15th March, 1890.

[2] Labadini calculates that a co-operative bake-house can save about 23 per cent. in comparison with other bake-houses. A new oven shown at the Milan International Bread-making Exposition, 1887, by Abate Orelli, with which for some reason Labadini does not deal, and which cost when finished 1300 *lire*, promised a saving of 35 per cent. on the expense of firing.

been already followed by certain bake-houses, and, among others, by that at Villanterio, cited farther back.

Since there has been much discussion as to the practical possibility of giving effect to sale at current prices, it is well to consider which of the two systems is most in vogue in different countries, reserving to myself the privilege of alluding elsewhere to the *results* of the different systems.

In England the societies which do not sell at current prices may be counted on one's fingers. It was only natural indeed, that the great prosperity of the Rochdale Society and the advantages springing from it should obscure the scant benefits of the other system of sale which drew on itself the by no means groundless hostility of traders.

In Germany the majority of societies sell at the mildest prices current, though many still sell at the lowest prices, in spite of the persistent counsels of Schulze and other apostles of co-operation. As long ago as 1868, Parisius (*Blätter für Genossenschaftswesen*), replying to those who pointed to the rapid strides of the Görlitz Society which sold at cost price, observed : " The supporters of the dividend principle (sale at current prices) have always given prominence to the fact, that in the experience which we have so far had of them, distributing co-operative societies which sell at the lowest prices, when conducted by able administrators, have progressed rapidly, but they have not forgotten another fact, that such co-operative societies, having reached a certain limit of business, stop in their development."

As regards France, M. Fongerousse, general Secretary of the French Co-operative Societies, and editor of *Les Coopérateurs Français*, speaking as the representative of the French Societies at the first Italian Co-operative Congress, said : " For me, for us Frenchmen, the question regarding the method of sale at the price current or at cost price is no longer in doubt, co-operate societies must sell at the retail price." The majority of those societies, in France as in Belgium, sell, as a matter of fact, at more than cost price.

In the United States the general council of the Sovereigns of Industry decided in 1877 to follow the Rochdale system in all its details ; and the decision appears to have been wisely carried out ; for some years later the chief secretary of the National Grange wrote : " Hundreds of societies of the Rochdale type have obtained complete success all over the country." And the general director of the " patrons of industry " referred as follows to 103 distributing societies in May, 1882 : " Our growth has astonished all alike. We have not had a single failure since the true Rochdale principle was acted on."

Italian experience, on the other hand, is often adduced to show the difficulties of sale at current prices. It is said that the Italian character, climate, habits, our economic conditions, are very different from those of England, that all institutions do not suit all peoples equally well; that, in short, the English system has met with ill success among us, and is not practicable.

Now no one can deny that each people have peculiar characteristics, but, luckily, it may be still doubted whether the Italians are so impatient and improvident that no one would become a member of a co-operative society, unless it enabled its members to obtain immediate benefits. Why, if others have succeeded, need we despair? It is not a question of trying a new method demanding efforts and sacrifices, but of profiting by the experience of others. If the two especial tendencies of the Italian character, which comprise its merits and defects, consist, as Turiello states, in a distinct and conscious individualism and the want of external discipline rendering every form of association difficult, must one therefore believe that confidence in co-operation is completely lacking, especially in a country where Schulze's "credit unions," transformed by Luzzati into people's banks with limited liability, have experienced a notoriously wide development?

But Italian experience proves very little against the English system, because, as Buffoli, a very able practical co-operator, said in 1886, "The true reason why the English system has not met with more success among us, is simply this, that it has never been applied in all its bearings."

A very efficient reason why the English system has not been followed in Italy is the unfortunate wording of Article 5 of the Act, 11th August, 1870, which was thus formulated:[1] "Co-operative societies are not bound to pay taxes on goods which they provide and distribute among their members exclusively for objects of beneficence."[2]

This article, "which does not sanction a privilege in favour of co-operative societies, but declares a right to be theirs," succeeded in some districts in its intention of promoting the formation of distributing societies, but distorted their true aim, by giving to them an artificial and too restricted a tendency.

[1] See on this article, besides the debates on the Chamber of Deputies, 1882, 1886, 1888, the reports of the three co-operative societies, and the Act, the monographs of Casella, *Una questione vitale per le società cooperative di consumo* (Caserta, 1886); and Guala, *La cooperazione e il dazio consumo* (Vercelli, 1886); and the two works of E. Pasquali, *Le società cooperative e la tassa di minuta vendita* (Torino, 1886); and *Le società cooperative in rapporto alle tasse di dazio consumo e di minuta vendita* (Torino, 1887).

[2] After many disputes it seems settled "that the object of beneficence in this matter, according to the intention of the legislator, is nothing but the distribution of goods carried on by means of the mere reimbursement of the expense of purchase and administration, excluding all speculation" (Sentence 21, January, 1888, of the Court of Cassation, Turin).

Owing to this article the rural co-operative societies of the Novara and Vercelli district sell at cost price and spread so rapidly, that while the "federation" of Novara presented itself at the first Italian Congress in 1886 with 24 societies, in 1887 it numbered 34; some of which, for example, Borgo Lavezzaro, Gravellona, Vernati, etc., did business at the rate of sixty, thirty, twenty thousand *lire* per annum. So far, I have been assured by A. Carotti, the soul of the Novarese co-operative movement, none of these societies show signs of a disposition to progress from their simple form to the more prolific Rochdale form.

But even in Italy the English system is not quite unknown, and it has also yielded very good results. Signor V. Armirotto, Secretary of the Sampierdarena Distributing Society, in 1883 thus wrote: "We have poor working-men who have put two or three *lire* into the society, and who, leaving alone the dividends, to-day have 500 *lire* and more in shares. Now as they are poor people, would they, if they had saved a few *centesimi* daily, have had this small capital, which at a given moment may be a real resource for them? Those who reply to this question, Yes! I account good theorists, but as having no practical knowledge of poor families and their needs."

A splendid as well as a more recent example is the Co-operative Union of Milan, which sells at the current market-prices. Buffoli, now President of the Union—

who had not succeeded in getting railway co-operative societies to adopt the Rochdale system, which was strenuously advocated by him—by his assiduous propaganda, assisted by a few well-wishers, succeeded in eradicating ancient Italian prejudices, in persuading people that co-operation should propose higher objects than a mere reduction of prices, that it must not aim at a present and ephemeral advantage so much as at a great advantage, destined to continue in the future: and thus he established the Co-operative Union, which has for its object the buying wholesale of cloth, drapery, and other articles in family use, in order to distribute them to its own members and the public (Art. 3 of the new statute approved by the Tribunal of Milan by the decree of 16th July, 1890). The results obtained by this society, called without exaggeration wonderful,[1] have shown that nothing precludes the

[1] In proof of this assertion I here adduce the eloquent figures supplied by the society's balance-sheet :—

Year.	Members.	Capital.	Sales.	Profits.
1886	387	110,950	17,086	11,058
1887	613	132,975	84,646	10,075
1888	874	140,925	231,026	24,836
1889	2127	388,125	681,539	82,250
1890(1st half)	2750	459,450	526,304	66,391

Among the members of the Union are more than 1000 ladies, to whom is due a large share of the credit for the progress of the society; because they constantly frequent the store and watch over its go'ngs on, attend the annual meetings, and on behalf of

success of the Rochdale system in Italy; and co-operators in other cities have decided to found analogous distributing societies on the same principles: and it is to be hoped that everywhere they may find able and

their society carry on an earnest propaganda which is most efficacious in augmenting the number of members, and thus enabling the store to make purchases in larger quantities and on better conditions. For the rest, the members of the Union belong to all classes in the city: persons who fill the highest public appointments, the most distinguished professional men and manufacturers, the highest officials of the magistracy and the public offices generally, together with the lowest door-keepers and poor working-men, who form their share by monthly instalments, are concerned in it. This freedom in admitting members of every class is sanctioned in Art. 4 of the new statute, by which all persons are allowed to form part of the society who have no interests antagonistic to those of the institution.

The sales now amount to over a hundred thousand *lire* monthly, and the reason why more is not made is the scantiness of the premises used for the sale. In September this year, the society will shift its quarters from Via Ugo Foscolo to the magnificent Palazzo Flori, near the Piazza del Duomo, where all the actual and existing departments will be materially enlarged by new departments, such as that for household furniture and articles of food. Afterwards special attention was paid to the setting up of a joint wine-cellar, for the carrying on of which there was appointed a suitable committee, who will be assisted in their labours by a responsible director and two vice-directors of tried experience and technical skill.

It is well to note—for the benefit of those traders who wish to detect financial privileges in favour of Italian co-operative societies which they do not enjoy—that the Union pays the maximum of the tax on trade, pays the weight and measure tax, the tax on movables, the room tax, the tax for exposing bills, for everything, in short, for which other traders pay taxes, and pays, in zealous administrators, as at Milan, that the force of excellent principles be not impaired through the inadequacy of individuals.

It is not true, then, that the English system is impracticable in Italy; many Italian societies, and especially the Union, demonstrate it.

But before quitting this subject it will be well to notice two observations recently made by Rava,[1] the champion of sale at cost price. After mentioning a polemic in which he had engaged with Buffoli, he writes: " In any case, as we had asserted that it behoved us to be content with the more direct advantages of distributing co-operative societies, *i.e.*, of their serving as a barrier to monopoly, and supplying to working-men bread and food of good quality at a

addition to these, the annual tax of 1·80 *lire* per cent. on the society's capital. Add to this that the Union, like other co-operative societies, but unlike other traders, enjoys the advantage of being compelled to pay invariably on the basis of the actual results of the balance-sheet, which, together with reports of the meetings and other documents, have to be presented to the tribunal on stamped paper, and then say whether co-operative societies flourish among us only through fiscal privileges granted them by the Government. The chief glory for the very rapid progress of the Co-operative Union is therefore due to the Council of Administration of this society, and especially to Sigg. L. Buffoli, L. Ponti and Dr. F. Guasti, who have formed part of the Council ever since November, 1886, and whose able, courageous and disinterested work no praise can sufficiently extol.

[1] *Le associazioni di mutuo soccorso e cooperative nelle provincie dell' Emilia*, Bologna, 1888.

cheap rate: as we had maintained that the shops and stores connected with mutual-aid societies were those which give the best promise of permanence and diffusion, we are glad that the data collected through the provinces of Emilia completely justify us."

It appears to me that in strictness the data do not completely justify Rava, and that, in order to prove it, it is enough to remember what Rabbeno[1] says of the little distributing society at Rivalta (a tiny fraction of the municipality of Reggio-Emilia), which has been in existence ever since 1873, and which gradually arose among the country-people by the saving of ten *centesimi* a week, by which shares were formed of six *lire;* it set out by borrowing in kind from its members some bags of grain; afterwards it started a sale; now it has also a pork factory, and its existence is assured, a success due to the Rochdale system, which it rigorously applied.

Rava's second observation is this: "Only when there are in Italy powerful organisations comparable to the English 'wholesales' (central distributing societies buying directly from producers in order to sell to distributing societies) shall we regard the carrying out of the Rochdale system as possible and useful." If Rava's remark were just and true, we might at once conclude that Italy must renounce the Rochdale system for ever, because the central societies evi-

[1] *Giornale degli economisti*, Bologna, gen. 1889.

dently find their *raison-d'être* in the smaller societies ("retail societies"), without which, especially their capital, they cannot exist; now since societies which sell at cost price, amassing no capital, will never be able to form a central society, nor will the others be able to do so—the formation of which, according to Rava, is neither possible nor useful—by whom, and how can these societies be constituted? Certainly by no one: unless, indeed, trampling upon the pure principles of co-operation, we are willing to have recourse to private beneficence or State intervention. Rava's observation cannot stand even a superficial criticism like this.

Let Italian distributing societies, therefore, be guided by the Co-operative Union of Milan, and remember that this society prefers sale at the price current to that at cost price, "because, while the latter would have at once attracted consumers, but obstructed all further progress, the former, on the contrary, permitted the society to form a capital of its own, by which, after doing away with the middlemen of commerce, it would be able to have recourse to the first sources of production, a capital which would be at all times a solid basis for the society, and by which it would be able to attain those lofty objects of moral and intellectual education which are the chiefest glory of English co-operative societies."[1]

[1] Report of the secretaries, Dr. Guasti and Sig. Albasini, at the

The idea of current market prices, of which I have spoken hitherto, needs to be better defined, because it is very wide. In England one set of co-operators champion sale at the highest prices, in order to obtain a very high dividend, while another supports sale at the mildest current prices. Tweddle, one of the "dividend hunters," in a conference held at Darlington, 1889, said: "Whether we wish it or not, the dividend is, and will continue for a long time to be, the greatest attraction of the co-operative movement for the major part of co-operators, and I know of no reason why we should condemn the natural desire to obtain the highest possible."

On the other hand, Hardly (? Hardy), one of the opponents, after maintaining that distributing co-operation should not be simply a gigantic commercial establishment for buying and selling, observed that "many members of co-operative societies do not earn so much as a pound a week, and cannot be forced to become co-operators."

Keeping prices very high, in order to increase the dividend among consumers, though it cannot, in the essentially free field of co-operation, be a form of compulsion to save, such as had fascinated certain exalted minds, like Laurand and Swift, may dissuade all those consumers from making purchases at co-

Cologne and Paris exhibitions, on the origins and development of the Union, rewarded by two gold medals in succession.

operative stores, who are not disposed to change distributing societies into savings' banks, where funds may be deposited under a new form, in order to obtain a very high interest. It is advisable, therefore, to sell at the mildest current prices.

In Italy, where many still admit only sale at cost price, and distributing societies, little diffused and not at all luxuriant, are modelled on very different systems, sale at the mildest prices current, in order that the societies may spread and become vigorous, is a necessity; moreover, those societies are not altogether to be condemned, which sell at a little lower than the current prices; at a rate, that is to say, which permits of a capital being formed enabling them to pass, later, to the best form of the English system. These societies, while showing at the outset the immediate advantages of co-operation, and slowly convincing people of the utility of its application, do not drag on a miserable existence from want of capital, and it is possible for them to progress and to adopt the Rochdale system later on.

(c) *On selling to non-members, and their participation in the profits.*

The question of selling to non-members is connected with that of prices. The co-operative societies which sell at cost price, with an addition for the expense of

administration, must exclude those who are not
members, those, that is to say, who have not helped
to form the society's capital. In exceptional cases,
and under given conditions, many of these societies
allow non-shareholders also to purchase.[1] But allowing non-shareholders to make purchases cannot be
compared with an unconditional sale to the public,
which, with sale at cost price, would resolve itself
into an act of beneficence. Nor can this beneficence
be avoided by selling to non-members at a higher
price than to members, without serious disorder and
confusion in the sale and the book-keeping, since it is

---

[1] The few English societies, not modelled on the Rochdale
type, sell not only to shareholders, but to annual subscribers,
i.e., to all those who pay five shillings the first year and half-a-
crown for succeeding years, in order to have the constant right
of purchasing at the society's store.

The co-operative society among the railway officials at Florence,
besides effective members, who must possess a share of 25 *lire*,
admits as associated members those officials who, being unwilling or unable to purchase a share, agree to contribute towards
keeping up the expense of the administration by paying a *lira*
every six months, besides a *lira* as entrance fee. They have
only the right of making purchases at the stores, and, therefore,
cannot vote in the meetings or take part in the distribution of
the eventual profits, and they are only admitted in limited
numbers decided by the council of directors. Associated members are also admitted in the co-operative store of the society
among railway officials at Turin. They pay one *lira* as entrance
fee and twenty *centesimi* a month as regular subscription. At
Iglesias the associated members pay 125 *lire* every six months;
at Siena six *lire* a year.

difficult to verify how many goods have been delivered to members, how many to non-members, and whether the purchaser is really a member or not; a difficulty which is almost insuperable when there is a large crowd of purchasers at the store, and which would occasion chaos in the administration and an easy wrecking of the institution.

The character of beneficence, on the other hand, does not necessarily attach to societies which sell at current prices, although it is observed that, with sale to non-members, societies depart from pure co-operative principles.[1] In practice, however, one cannot be bound by theoretical conceits, and institutions which do not proceed by rules of logic must adapt themselves to the suitability of one form rather than another. Co-operative societies, which sell to non-members, either gain something or nothing on the sale, or else lose by it: on the first hypothesis, the society assumes a mixed co-operative-speculative character; on the third, it becomes partly a benefit institution; on the second, the type of co-operation is, if not purely identical with those which sell to members only, on a par with them. It is needful, therefore, to see whether this sale to non-members, without gain or benefit, is opportune, since no one will wish, for the sake of a

[1] In a proposition at the second Congress of Italian co-operators, the phrase was approved: "It is consonant with the nature of co-operation that goods be distributed to members only."

theoretical principle, to oppose a practical application, which is not very far removed from the pure form of co-operation, when its utility is evident.

Practically, it is impossible to stop purchases being made at the society on account of strangers, that is to say, members re-selling the goods of the institution to others, thus making it of no use to many persons to belong directly to the society. Many members, to avoid the increase in the members being thus stopped, have threatened to expel any member making purchases for others: instead of this measure, which is too serious and difficult to carry into effect, other societies (as, for instance, that at Nugola, near Pisa) have ordered a fine in the case of the member who shall make purchases over and above the needs of his own family. This, however, is no security against sale to non-members taking place, as it is not a sure preventive to adopt signs of recognition (tokens or tickets) for members, which are of no service where, from their large numbers, members may safely transfer the tokens to non-members.

Experience, especially foreign experience, teaches that it is very advantageous for co-operative societies not to sell to members only. Sale to the public convinces all of the good quality and just measure of the goods, gives great publicity to the co-operative society, whose advantages every one may easily ascertain for himself, and helping on one of the objects of co-operation, that of extending its benefits as fully as possible, it permits consumers, without trouble, to get the best articles at the proper weight and measure.

The sole inconvenience in the sale to non-members is the difficulty of ascertaining the needs of a body of customers who have no permanent interest in buying at the joint-store, which necessitates a skill and foresight common in traders, but which is often wanting in co-operators. But it is well to notice that even with exclusive sale to members it is not always possible to make a perfect calculation between purchases and sales, for often enough members do not deal exclusively with the society, and the risk of warehousing some goods and of being unprovided with others may be very slight, if affairs are conducted with prudence.

It is often discussed whether societies, which sell at current prices, ought, on accounts being made up, to distribute a share of the profits to non-members.

As against such distribution it has been remarked: when a person has no interest in the society, and risks in it neither money nor labour, by what right or with what appearance of justice would he share the savings of the society? Because, forsooth, he is a regular customer and contributes to the prosperity of the business? But unless he had found his account in buying at the joint-stores, he would not have made purchases in them. Another argument is this: if purchasers, not being members, share in the dividend, the number of members will dwindle, or, at any rate, will not grow, because if a person who has contributed nothing to the society, and is responsible for nothing, enjoys the same advantages as one who risks something or invests his own exertions, no one will feel any desire to belong to this society.

It is easy to reply to these arguments.

To distributing societies, unlike other societies, the purchaser brings greater advantages than the capitalist: a distributing society, as an enterprise, differs, that is to say, from the ordinary enterprise, in that it is carried out by the patrons of the enterprise themselves. The society requires that the goods purchased should be sold, and the buyers, not being members who favour this sale, help to obtain savings; and if they contribute to them, why should they not share in the division of them?

Further, buyers not being members, who purchase at market prices, pay something in addition to what the goods cost the society; and would it not be an open injustice, would it not be changing the society from a co-operative into a speculative one, if it did not return to all its customers, without distinction, what they have paid in excess? Restitution of savings is only an act of justice in the case of any one who has paid more than he really ought.[1]

[1] Thus, for example, the *Biene* of Berlin, which sells to the

CO-OPERATIVE SOCIETIES.

Naturally the net profits ought not to be divided per head among all the consumers, members and non-members; members, who have risked capital and have social duties, cannot with justice be treated like non-members. True co-operation ought to divide the advantages proportionally, not equally, among those who have produced them; and when the members have received a quota as compensation for capital invested, distribution is made to all consumers in proportion to what each has consumed.

As regards the expediency of this distribution of savings to non-members, Nazzani writes: "Stores which have adopted this system have profited by it: they have attracted many consumers, added to their gains, and accustomed poor people to co-operation who had not even wherewithal to pay the entrance fee. If you wish to extend the sale, if you wish to attract patrons to the joint-store, you must attract them by participation in the profits, for otherwise they will not come in large numbers, particularly through the difficulty of paying ready money. Do not say that in this way consumers are kept from

public, but divides the profits only among those consumers who are members, is not purely co-operative. This society does not carry on a large business, since, after 25 years of life, it sold n 1888 only to the amount of 375,000 *lire* and had 2743 members; while the Milan *Unione*, which distributes its profits among all consumers, after only three years, sold in 1889 to the extent of 681,539 *lire*.

becoming members, and that on these conditions almost every one would be satisfied with being a customer. In the first place, it is the members who deliberate and administer — they are the masters. Then, again, they receive an interest from their shares; and, finally, they can withhold the quotas of dividend due to non-members, until they have determined their contributions to the society.

The restitution of savings to non-members is the best means of convincing people by facts of the usefulness of co-operative societies. Vague promises of possible advantages meet with many unbelievers; but when the consumer, as patron, receives a part of the profits, he begins assiduously to cater for himself in the stores, where he can only gain, and runs no risk of loss. Little by little the patron thinks seriously of the advantages of co-operation, and ends by joining. If consumers are attracted by important, solid, and evident interest, there will be few opposers of co-operation.

English societies of the Rochdale type, in order to induce patrons to join more, do not distribute the savings to consumers, members, and non-members, by the same rule, but give to non-members half or two-thirds of what they give to members; so that, for example, if 10 per cent. is given to members on their purchases, 5 or $7\frac{1}{2}$ per cent. is given to non-members, the remainder going to the reserve fund or other objects exclusive of gain.

Some societies resolve that only associates shall share in the 60 per cent. of the profits assigned to purchasers; but all purchasers, not being associates, who shall demand their admittance twenty days before the general meeting, which is to settle the dividends on the working, shall share in the profits proportionally to their consumption with other members.

These arrangements clearly aim at augmenting the number of members.

Practically, ascertaining the quantity of goods consumed by each patron presents no serious difficulty. Various methods have been suggested for it.

In England each society has a certain number of counters of different value, from fivepence to half a sovereign. The patrons who purchase to the amount of a shilling receive a counter of the value of a shilling. These counters, which are saved up by members, must be given back when they reach a certain figure; when added together they express the amount of purchases made by each member, and thus enable the respective quota of saving to be determined. These counters present two inconveniences: first and foremost, the counters used being almost always of zinc or brass instead of paper, which is easily torn, they mean a considerable expense to the society; further, they allow the possessors to sell them to some other purchaser from the society, in order to obtain forthwith, at least in part, the small savings represented by the counters.

Another method also is a good deal used. The co-operative society supplies every patron, whether a member or a non-member, with a memorandum-book, in order that there may be entered in it, and the day-book of the society, every purchase made at the store; at the moment of balancing the sums registered in it are made up. This system is not very inconvenient in the shop, and in fact many business houses use it for sale on credit retail. Other methods are treated of by Signor Ponti in his *Manuale per le società di consumo*.

Here it suffices us to point out a new contrivance invented by Mr. Knight, which serves to mark the amount of the purchase with rapidity and precision on the paper counter or certificate of purchase (mother and daughter). Perhaps it would be advisable to introduce this contrivance into Italian co-operative stores, although the system of purchase certificates, called also checks, is not without inconveniences. Where, that is to say, the sales are immense, as is generally the case in England, and the daily issue of these certificates is very great, in a little while their progressive number exceeds a large figure, which renders registration and control difficult. This inconvenience co-operative societies can themselves remedy by dividing the checks into several series. Last January, therefore, Mr. Thirlaway proposed that the checks should be numbered from 1 to 6,000, putting the number of the series under the progressive number of the check.

Generally speaking, every concern discovers a way of adapting such systems to its own needs and those of its patrons.

(d) How the capital is formed and the profits distributed.

Three elements ought especially to be considered in distributing societies :—

1st. The buying price of the products.

2nd. The expense of administration and the accessory expenses of the society.

3rd. The formation and increase of the society's capital, which is necessary, in order that the society may attain those objects for which it has been constituted.

These elements enter into the price which the member pays for the products which are distributed to him, into the capital paid, into the entrance fee which is paid for co-partnership in the reserve fund, etc.

Although, in order to form a distributing society, we need consumers before capital, nevertheless a share, however small, of capital is necessary in order to start the undertaking.

The capital is sometimes formed by payments to a sinking fund, or by unproductive quotas: in this case the unproductive (not however gratuitous) contribution does not form an anti-economic fact, because it represents an amount expended in order to enjoy determinate advantages by means of the society thus constituted.

More often the capital is formed by small periodical contributions, compulsory on members, which subsequently give rise to shares.[1] With us, by Art. 224 Commercial Code, shares are limited to 100 *lire*, but usually they are much lower in order to render the acquisition of them easy to small fortunes. It is advisable, however, that the dimensions of the shares should not be too small, so as to make the formation of a capital difficult, since, in addition to that, it is evident that, owing to registration and stamp duty, the share capital of societies, which have shares of

---

[1] In order to save distributing societies from stamp-duty on share certificates, Sig. Manfredi, in the second Italian Congress, proposed the following order of the day, which was approved:—
"The Congress recommends that the new statutes be extended, and the existing ones modified in such a way that, as the result, the capital may be collected, not by shares, but by small subscriptions, certified only by the books of the society, without any mention of shares." This expedient of suppressing the word "share" in order to escape the unjust imposition of a tax, was condemned on the ground that co-operative societies ought not to evade any law; to this observation, however, Manfredi and others returned a satisfactory answer.

very small dimensions, will be more heavily taxed than the others.[1]

In regard to the paying of the shares it is expedient to follow the English system, *i.e.*, of not allowing members to draw the quotas of saving falling to them, until they have definitively paid the subscribed shares. To this useful restriction it will be proper to make an exception by empowering the council of administration to re-imburse the whole or part of his interest in the society to a member who, from illness or some other adversity, pays under embarrassing circumstances.

In the case of societies which have attained to a considerable development, there often arises the danger of a plethora of capital. When the society cannot employ all the capital which it has to dispose of in its own business, it must set bounds to its excessive abundance, if it does not wish to be wanting in its office. In England, where members, accustomed to thriftiness, tend to increase the savings by leaving them in the societies, which sufficiently provided with capital, did not know what to do with them, this danger has been confirmed. Various expedients were considered for avoiding it, whilst it was sought to

[1] There are, among us, shares of 10 *lire* (Trivero Vandano), of 70 (Mosso S. Maria), of 25 (Milan *Unione*), of 15 (Quinzano), of 12 (Altavilla Irpino), of 6 (Venice), 5 (Delianova di Reggio, Calabria), of 1 (Siena).

preserve in the employment of capital a co-operative character: building societies were organised, a development was given to assurance societies, considerable sums were devoted to the education of members, and lastly, the societies devoted themselves directly to production; but, nevertheless, the abundance of capital in certain societies is so considerable that some were obliged, like that at Leeds, to reduce the statutory interest on the capital from 5 to 4 per cent.

Other English societies (*Army and Navy, Civil Service, Supply Association, New Civil Service*), not of the Rochdale type, in order to preclude this danger, have a limited capital: but this arrangement impedes the continuous progress of the society, by excluding from it new elements suited to maintain that co-operative tendency which, restricted to a few persons, easily degenerates into a speculative one, and renders an organisation adapted to old and new needs impossible.

With greater sense and prudence the Milan *Unione Co-operativa*, at the end of the year 1888, after two years' existence, alarmed at the rapid increase of capital, which threatened to be out of proportion to the needs of the society, thought of according to the meeting of members the right to determine from year to year the highest limit of the shares, which each member might purchase: for 1889, as for 1890, the highest limit was fixed at four shares. Now that the

Unione has rented the Palazzo Floii, where it occupies an area of 3000 square *mètres*, instead of the 800 which it formerly occupied, and must lay out new capital, it has raised the limit to twenty shares.

In order to avoid this plethora, some have recommended societies which have a sale of their own to immobilise part of their capital in purchases, or the construction of premises for the use of the society. But this remedy also is not without danger, since, in moments of crises, societies in this condition can with difficulty meet the demands of members, thus by refusal of payment adding to the members' fear, and accelerating the ruin of the society. In England, despite the large investment of capital in premises on the part of co-operative societies, this danger is reduced by the infrequency of crises, and the solidity and solidarity of these societies: the Rochdale Society, in a moment of panic, was saved from ruin by the ability and firmness of its administrators, who paid the first demands for the restitution of quotas completely and without hesitation, and thus the confidence of the members was renewed.

In Italy many co-operative societies, instead of the danger of plethora, are in want of capital. Some societies, especially in southern Italy, through the exertions of that shrewd and able co-operator, O. Casella, have used an ingenious means for attracting capital and fostering, at the same time, habits of thrift, by adopting a particular method of saving which offers an important gain. There is deposited with the society a *soldo* (the minimum) a day, and the society at the end of the year restores twenty *lire:* while five *centesimi* a day would yield at the end of the year (0·05 × 365) 18·25 *lire*, the society gives in addition 1·75 *lire*, which is equivalent to interest of 12 per cent. and more, that is, three times as much as is given by the best institutions of credit. Thus the society, while by a very high interest it promotes saving, can dispose of a larger capital, and does not lose by it, since it employs this deposit in the purchase of consumable articles which, under ordinary circumstances, offer good compensation on account of the rapid circulation of capital.

An important difference between co-operative and other share-holding societies is the limitation of the quota, which each member can possess in a distributing society, fixed in our commercial code at 5000 *lire*, the design being to prevent some rich capitalist from absorbing the greater part of the joint capital, so that the other small shareholders are of little or no importance.

On the hypothesis that the society does not sell at cost price, it is possible to speak of the distribution of profits, and only in regard to these societies, is it necessary to enter on the difficult subject of this distribution.

If the society, having paid the expenses, designs all that remains over for the indivisible joint capital, there is no more to be said about the division of profits. This system adopted by rural co-operative lending banks, might be adopted also by distributing societies, especially in small rural municipalities. "It would appear to us," writes Gobbo, "equally erroneous to say that this system is unjust, and to declare that it alone conforms to the co-operative principle. Members agree to pay something extra on the price of the product, in order to form the capital of an institution, which they regard as permanently advantageous to their families; and so they do not make a sacrifice on account of this, since the founding of an association strikes them as a less costly form of obtaining products, than having recourse to traders; in like manner they agree to let other families of the municipality avail themselves of it, who did not join the association at the outset. It is rather the feeling of the solidarity of interests among all the families of the municipality than a real act of beneficence: or anyhow it is an almost imperceptible trace of beneficence."

On the other hand, this system cannot be recommended in an absolute way: where there is not that disposition of mind on the part of the members, it will still be necessary to put together the joint capital, but a capital of which the member or his heirs may draw the quota falling to them in such cases as the statute provides, and of which the new members must put together their quota. This result is obtained by compelling members to leave alone the share of savings assigned to them until their quota of capital has been made up.

When societies sell at a price such as to enable, after expenses have been paid, a capital to be formed, this is distributed, in whole or in part, to the members in proportion to the products consumed. The gains of the society are true and proper profits, since they are the strict result of the three elements which determine them—*i.e.*, recompense for the capital employed, remuneration for the work of direction, administration, and oversight, and compensation for the risk of the enterprise. The highness of these profits, in societies with sale at cost price, can be estimated by comparing the price of goods at the store with that of other shops. In societies which sell at current prices the distribution of gains at the end of the year is not merely distribution of profits: the profit occurs when the member purchases the commodity at the store, and if the member, instead of wishing for this profit immediately, leaves it in the society's chest, his quota of profit is, as it were, a deposit of saving, so that one cannot with any accuracy describe it as a distribution of profits or returns[1] in speaking of the distribution of

[1] The question, whether co-operative societies ought or ought not to pay the tax on moveable property, is now almost solved

these societies' gains after balancing, just as it is impossible to term return or profit that amount which a person might receive at the end of the year by bringing his daily saving to the savings' bank.

in Italy. With respect to stores worked by a mutual aid society, the law of 15th April, 1886, is explicit (Art. 9): "Mutual aid societies, when registered, enjoy . . . exemption . . . from the tax on moveable property." When the society sells at a price augmented by what is necessary to cover expenses, it is impossible to speak of returns, and, consequently, of taxes. When the society distributes the profits after balancing, it only reimburses to members that in excess of the cost price which they paid at the moment of purchasing the goods : it is, therefore, a restitution of savings and not a return.

Signor Zanardelli, questioned on the point by Buffoli, said: "The net gain resulting from the balance-sheet of a co-operative store cannot be termed returns, and only the interest on the sums saved and capitalised is subject to taxation." This same principle was admitted by the Central Commission for direct taxation in the final decisions (without appeal), under date 26th May, 1878, No. 49,382, 30th October, 1879, No. 56,504, and 30th May, 1885, No. 79,887. The Central Commission held that "it is immaterial that the members, in order to facilitate accounts, pay in the first place what is paid by strangers, and that there is afterwards refunded to them what they are ascertained to have paid over and above the cost price, it being evident that this does not constitute a dividend of gains, but rather the refunding of capital before paid."

The revenue officer at Caserta has shrewdly observed, à propos of this, that there is not merely a restitution of savings, since the member receives a portion of the profits made on all the commodities, even if the commodity consumed by him eventually produced a loss to the society. Here is his example: "The society has purchased wine for 1000 lire, but, in consequence of this having gone wrong, it has sold it at a loss of 200 lire. How-

Before distributing the net gains to consumers, almost all societies give the quota which falls to it to the capital. For the most part, there is assigned to the capital a fixed percentual quota which is neither interest nor profit (dividend), and has the drawbacks of both without possessing their advantages, because it is fixed beforehand, like the interest of borrowed capital, without payment of it being assured when there are no profits, and it runs all the risks of the dividend without the prospect of increasing when the profits of the business are on the increase. Thus, English co-operative societies in their statutes gener-

ever, on the whole, it has had on the sale of the other commodities a profit of 1200 *lire*, which, after deducting the said 200, become 1000. Let us imagine that these 1000 *lire* proceed from a sale of 100,000 *lire*, including the sale of the wine lost. One has to restore to the consumers, therefore, 1 per cent., consequently 8 *lire* to the member purchasing wine. Are these 8 *lire* what has been paid in excess? Are they the difference between the buying and selling price? Evidently not." In practice, however, this difference may be ignored, although, theoretically, a system of book-keeping might be discovered which should eliminate this as well.

If the society sold to members and non-members, and distributed what was paid in excess to all the purchasers in proportion to the purchases made by each of them, it would not alter the substance of the question, because it would be still a simple restitution of a greater outlay, and thus the tax on moveable property could not be applied.

The moveable property, therefore, will have to pay on the dividends to the capital and the other sums assigned to the joint capital.

ally assign 5 per cent. to the capital, and many French societies imitate them.

Through the influence of socialistic theories, there is sometimes refused any quota to the capital: it is a notorious doctrine of the socialists that only the labour of the workman is productive, and that interest, which is nothing but a forced and cruel stipulation between robbing capital and the workman robbed, is unjust. This well-known socialist theory, impugned by many, has had an effect on many societies in the assigning of no quota, or a very small quota, to the capital.[1]

Apart from these theories, the discussion of which would demand some volumes, there are no adequate reasons for refusing to the capital a quota equal to the current interest, or even somewhat larger than that, in order to compensate the risk of those who employ capital in these societies, for, however slight, it is always greater than that of people who deposit money in a savings' bank. Lastly, it will be well, in order to avoid in practice capital prevailing over consumption[2] in the distribution of

[1] The Austrian economic school combats this theory in detail. See, for instance, Böhm-Bawerk, *Geschichte und Kritik der Kapitalzins Theorieen.* Innsbruch, 1884.

[2] The *Hebden Bridge Manufacturing Society*, in the first half-year of 1889, excited very lively protests on the part of English co-operators for having given to the capital a dividend corresponding to 71·2 per cent.—*i.e.*, for having made an anti-cooperative distribution.

profits, to fix a maximum for this quota in the statute.[1]

Besides assigning a quota to the capital, co-operative societies are warmly recommended to constitute a reserve fund. This is, so to speak, an assurance fund which prevents recourse being had to the joint-capital in case of some loss, and ought, therefore, to be greater, the greater the risks of the society: thus, it is very imprudent, for instance, to devote oneself to production without a strong reserve fund.

The reserve fund, being designed to remedy eventual losses as a subsidiary capital independent of members, must not be looked upon as the property of the members only, but of all the consumers, when the society sells to the public; and, therefore, in case of dissolving, it cannot, in accordance with justice, be divided among the members only. And it is thanks to this capital, put by little by little, that it will be possible, perhaps, for an aspiration to be realised thus expressed by Luzzati:—" And why, with kindled fancy, cannot one have glimpses of a distant period, in which the reserve fund may equal and exceed the capital paid by members and allow of a gradual refunding of it, thus creating a common and indivisible patrimony in the interest of public credit?"

In the distribution of the net gains, after having

[1] The Milan *Unione* has fixed its maximum limit at 6 per cent.

assigned one quota to the capital and one to the reserve fund, it is advisable to assign a share also to the manager and the rest of the *personnel*, that they may be interested and aroused to press forward the welfare of the society. The remainder of the profits is distributed to the purchasers in proportion to their consumption, the members being obliged to leave alone their share of such gains until the quota of capital, which they are to distribute, has been made up.

Very many co-operative societies also set apart a percentage of these gains for a co-operative propaganda, or establishing an educational fund, or life assurances, or a pension fund, or forming central distributing societies, building, manufacturing societies, etc. Here the remark will be applicable, "*Usus te plura docebit,*" so numerous are the ways by which a distributing society, having capital at command, can better the condition of the needy classes: ways which are all completely closed to those societies which sell at cost price.

How certain countries show a special tendency to follow one or the other of these methods, will be seen in the sequel.

CHAPTER VI.

SPREAD OF DISTRIBUTING CO-OPERATIVE SOCIETIES.

England.

DISTRIBUTING societies have got on better in England than in any other country. Since I am not writing the history of distributing societies, I do not stay to speak fully of the Rochdale Society, the first distributing society [1] in the world, notices of which, usually taken from Holyoake's History, are found in all books dealing with co-operative societies, and I confine myself simply to giving the most recent *data* regarding this celebrated society.

[1] First in point of time, for, in spite of the existence of a distributing society at York in 1795 having been discovered, it cannot be denied that the first true co-operative society, which has served and still serves as a pattern throughout the world, is that of Rochdale. Certainly, *natura non facit saltus*, and an organic and complex institution like that of Rochdale cannot have arisen all at once without precedents. Still it is impossible on that account to identify those germs and those incomplete forms of co-operation, to judge by which, as Robert Owen wrote, co-operative societies go back to 1696, and, perhaps, further, with a true co-operative society.

The *Rochdale Equitable Pioneer Society* (*Limited*), formed by 28 flannel-weavers with £28 sterling, started a shop in December, 1844, for selling to members and non-members goods, bought wholesale, at the current prices of the town. The shop was open in the evening only, and the committee and other members were the distributors. The statute then drawn up is, with slight modifications, still in force. What the progress of the society has been from its origin to the end of 1889, will appear from the following table:—

Year.	Members.	Capital	Sale.	Net Profits.
1844	28	£28	£ —	—
1845	74	181	710	£22
1846	80	252	1,146	80
1847	110	286	1,924	72
1848	149	397	2,276	117
1854	900	7,172	33,374	1,763
1864	4,747	62,105	174,937	22,717
1874	7,639	192,814	298,888	40,679
1875	8,415	225,682	305,657	48,212
1876	8,892	254,000	305,190	50,668
1877	9,722	280,275	311,754	51,648
1878	10,187	292,344	298,679	52,694
1879	10,427	288,035	270,072	49,751
1880	10,613	292,570	283,655	48,545
1881	10,697	302,151	272,142	46,242
1882	10,894	315,243	274,627	47,608
1883	11,050	326,875	276,456	51,599
1884	11,161	329,470	262,270	50,268
1885	11,084	324,645	252,072	45,254
1886	10,984	321,678	246,031	44,111
1887	11,152	328,100	256,736	46,047
1888	11,278	344,669	267,726	47,119
1889	11,342	353,470	270,685	47,263

It is useful to indicate how the Rochdale administrators have employed the capital in excess of the society's requirements. The society devoted itself to the production of objects of consumption in 1854; in 1867 it built its central store in Toad Lane at the cost of £14,000; then it built or purchased twenty-four other shops in different parts of the town for the greater convenience of purchasers; it established an assurance society against fires and against losses of the society through the dishonesty of officials and servants, and founded a sick and burial club.

In order to promote instruction, the society has set apart $2\frac{1}{2}$ per cent. of the net profits for educational objects; the school founded by it has now more than 450 scholars. It has, moreover, a library of its own, consisting of 17,081 volumes, a large reading-room ("news-room") and nineteen smaller rooms, supplied with the most important journals and reviews of all countries. In order to accustom the young to economy and prudence, it allows them exceptionally favourable conditions for the employment of small capital. Moreover, the society lends money to members under a hypothetical guarantee and within certain limit (Art. 49 and 50 of the Statute), for the purchase of a site or the purchase or building of houses for their own habitation: and often the building department builds directly, acting as a true building co-operative society.

The Rochdale Society is not alone in affording such a host of advantages, but almost all societies of the Rochdale type are very prosperous and present advantages equal to, and sometimes greater than, these. Here, also, before speaking of the advantages of English societies in general, let me quote a particular case.

In Halifax there exists a distributing society which sells nearly all the articles necessary for a family. It has made a contract with a manufacturer by means of which it furnishes its members with the means of "economizing" a house on their consumption. The manufacturer sells the site, the society advances the funds for the purchase of the site and the building of the cottages and reimburses itself on the annual dividends of the members. It was estimated that a family of work-people in Yorkshire, composed of a husband, wife and four children, consumes on an average as much as is sufficient to become owner at the end of fourteen years of a pretty cottage. "A consumption," writes Ludlow, " which leads to immoveable property, *houses which are bought by eating*, here, you must allow, are economic paradoxes which Smith and Léon Say assuredly did not foresee."

A table taken from the *Co-operative Wholesale Societies' Annual* for 1890 enables us to show briefly the movement of English co-operative societies of the Rochdale type, especially during the last few years.

Year.	No. of Registered Societies	No. of Members.	Capital in Shares at the end of each year.	Sales.	Nett Profits.	Profits devot'd to Educational Objects.
1862	332	90,341	£428,376	£2,333,523	£165,562	—
1872	935	330,350	2,969,573	13,012,120	936,715	£6,696
1882	1288	687,158	7,591,241	27,541,212	2,155,398	14,778
1883	1291	729,957	7,921,356	29,336,028	2,434,996	16,788
1884	1400	797,950	8,646,188	30,424,101	2,723,794	19,154
1885	1441	850,659	9,211,259	31,305,910	2,988,690	20,712
1886	1486	864,488	9,747,452	32,730,745	3,070,111	19,878
1887	1516	967,828	10,344,216	34,483,771	3,190,309	21,380

In order duly to estimate the importance of these data it is well to observe that these official statistics show the registered societies only (in 1887, for example, the non-registered societies were 145, so that the number of societies actually in existence was 1661), and that each member is ordinarily the father of a family, from which, estimating on an average every family as composed of four members and the present number of members at about a million, it results that about four millions of English feel the advantages of co-operative societies, beside those who, without being members, procure from them objects of consumption.

In 1887 every member saved on an average 82 *lire*. The total sales in the 25 years from 1862 to 1887 amounted to 10,851,504,650 Italian *lire*, with net profits of 905,499,525 Italian *lire*. Certainly none are so blind as those who won't see, but these nine hundred and five millions saved in the interest of the less comfortable classes,[1] and the constant progress of co-operative societies which is evidenced by the table shown, demonstrate how inaccurate were the assertions of Leroy-Beaulieu and Hubert-Valleroux[2] who affirmed that co-operation is an idea which has gone out of fashion and which barely survives.

Besides societies of the Rochdale type, there are others which do not sell at the current market prices. The first—the Civil Service—arose in this way. Three young officials of the English Post Office observed: "We alone consume in a month a box of tea which we might buy at the docks at 6 *lire* per pound, while the retail dealer makes us pay 7 *lire*." They bought therefore a chest of tea and divided it between them in equal shares. The information having spread among their colleagues, there was speedily established the first store of the *Civil Service*, which was quickly followed by the *Supply Association, Civil Service Co-operative, New Civil Service Co-operation*, and in 1871 the *Army and Navy*, with its branch, the *Army and Navy Auxiliary*, founded in 1882. The following is the amount of the sales in these stores during the whole of 1889:—

---

[1] According to a calculation of Ludlow, three quarters of the members are working-men.
[2] *Les associations coopératives en France et à l'étranger*, Paris, 1884.

Civil Service Co-operative Stores	£481,110
Army and Navy	2,619,298
New Civil Service	151,648
Junior Army and Navy	576,069
Army and Navy Auxiliary	524,124
Civil Service Supply Association	1,852,166
Harrad's Stores	492,542

These societies sell to share-holding members, annual subscribers and life-members—if there are any—but the profits are divided among the shareholders only. This system clearly departs from true co-operative principles, inasmuch as it assigns too much to the capital; but it is impossible to assert with some that these societies cannot prosper, since, for instance, the *Army and Navy* sells to the extent of about 200 thousand Italian *lire* a day and has a capital of about 30 million *lire:* it is, however, to be observed that this society does not sell at the cost price augmented by expenses, but at a price permitting the formation of a capital, and puts from 12 to 15 per cent. on the commodities, thus tolerably approximating to the current prices.

Apropos of English co-operation, it is requisite to speak of central distributing societies.

The smallness of the sums which distributing societies have at their command, prevents large provisions being obtained wholesale at the most favourable season, and stops, therefore, recourse being had directly to producers. When, in one district, there exists several distributing co-operative societies, the wish easily arises of coming to a mutual understanding for eliminating wholesale traders, and, if possible, establishing a wholesale depot in order to carry on reserve trading there; thus saving for their united benefit the gains of the wholesale traders.

In practice various ways are indicated for satisfying this wish.

1st. The combination of several co-operative societies for the joint purchase of goods wholesale.

2nd. One co-operative society sells its own goods to others.

3rd. One co-operative society buys goods on commission for others.

4th. The combination of several co-operative societies for establishing a central society to buy and sell wholesale as an independent society (*wholesale society, Waaren-Engroshandlung-Gesellschaft*).

The choice of one or other of these modes depends on a number of particular circumstances which are met with in practice, and which explain the different forms taken by these agreements in different countries.

When the English societies were convinced of the usefulness, not only of distributing goods purchased from merchants and producers in free competition, but of transforming *themselves* into merchants and producers, there arose two wholesale co-operative societies. The first, the English, with its seat at

Manchester, commenced business on its own account on 14th March, 1864; the other, the Scotch, with its seat at Glasgow, in September, 1868. Here, taken from their statutes, are the fundamental rules on which they are governed.

All co-operative societies admitted by the general committee may be members of the "wholesales," provided they are registered in accordance with the *Industrial and Provident Societies' Act, 1876*, and the various *companies with Limited Liability Acts*, or according to the law of the country in which they are, so long as they can trade as independent societies. (Profiting by this arrangement the *Unione* has joined the English "wholesale.")

Each affiliated society must purchase not less than one share of £5 for every ten of its members (Art. 5 of the English *whol.*), or not less than one share of 15 shillings for each member (Art. 6 of the Scotch *whol.*), the number rising with the increase of members.

Every society at the moment of its admission must pay not less than a tenth of the shares subscribed, but no dividend or interest is calculated on the share not fully paid.

The advantages of the member societies are, 1st, each society receives double the quota of dividend on the purchases granted to buyers not being members;[1]

[1] Hence, it is evident that these societies do not sell at cost price now to members only, as some Italian writers believe.

2nd, the capital in shares is returned in a proportion not greater than 5 per cent. a year ; 3rd, the societies share in the administration in proportion to the amount of their purchases, and have a right to vote in the special and general meetings.

Goods must be paid for within seven days of the date of the invoice; after a delay of fourteen days the society refuses to execute any further order of the tardy society until the first debt has been paid. The prices are made known by the weekly publication of the price-list, distributed to the retail societies *gratis*. Besides the respite alluded to, in order to remove difficulties and inconveniences on the part of distant societies in forwarding coin, and to promote the safe and productive employment of money, the Manchester " wholesale " in 1872 established a *Bank Department*, while the Glasgow Society availed itself of the Union Bank of Scotland for the transmission of cheques. Both " wholesales " have several branches also.

Through the spread and development of the retail societies, through the uniformity of their constitution, and on account of the peculiar topographical conditions of England, these societies met with splendid success. At present these societies have branches for wholesale purchases at Rouen, Calais, Copenhagen, New York, etc, and for goods' transport abroad possess five vessels in their exclusive service. The following view which completes that drawn up by

Rabbeno down to 1883, in his very well-known book on Co-operation in England, indicates the constant advance :—

Year.	Capital.		Sales.		Net Profits.	
	English.	Scotch.	English.	Scotch.	English.	Scotch.
	£	£	£	£	£	£
1884	701,358	244,186	4,675,371	1,300,331	54,491	29,435
1885	841,175	288,946	4,793,151	1,438,220	77,630	39,641
1886	944,379	333,653	5,223,179	1,857,152	83,328	50,398
1887	1,017,042	367,309	5,713,235	1,810,015	65,141	47,278
1888	1,116,035	409,608	6,200,074	1,963,853	82,490	53,538
		1st half year.		1st half year.		1st half year.
1889	—	453,835	—	1,078,557	—	30,501

Altogether the English "wholesale" from 1864 to the end of 1888, had had in net profits 19,992,350 Italian *lire*, and the Scotch, from 1868, 10,783,350 Italian *lire*.

Besides these two economic centres there is also, to use Rabbeno's expression, a "psychical centre," which is the *Co-operative Union, Limited*, established in 1873 at the Newcastle Congress, "in order practically to promote honesty, justice, and economy in production and exchange." It is not, therefore, an institution exclusively for distributing societies, but owing to the small importance of other forms of co-operation in England, it may be said that it operates only in regard to these.

The executive organ of this Union is the *Central Board*, which is,

1st. An office for legal and administrative advice on every subject of interest to the societies.

2nd. An office of statistics which collects all sorts of information for the free use of societies, to whom it may be of service.

3rd. A propaganda agency for the spread of co-operative principles in Great Britain and Ireland, and in all the world.

Co-operative and commercial societies belong to it. No society is admitted until it has declared that it will be subject to the rules shown to it, by which it must be guided in all its affairs, and until it has made the annual payment in the following way :—

(a) If the societies number less than 500 members, the sum is twopence per member.

(b) If the number of members exceeds 500, the lowest sum is 1000d. In reckoning the number of members, if one society includes others, each society is considered a member.

Although the Union has a purely moral authority, it is most efficacious. It represents the entire co-operative movement, and prepares the labours of the annual congresses. A propaganda carried on in all kinds of ways and so as to suit all classes of persons, is the most usual means for attaining its object. In this it is powerfully aided by the *Co-operative News,* a journal published by a federation of co-operative societies. This journal of 16 pages regularly devotes

2 pages to women in the *Women's Corner*. Women, who may be members of co-operative societies with the right of voting, have formed a special league—the *Women's Guild for the Spread of Co-operation*.

The annual co-operative congresses, in which very eminent men[1] do not disdain to take part, have no immediate importance, or one which can be indicated by figures, but their usefulness cannot, therefore, be mistaken. A common study of the annual co-operative movement, the tendency to co-operate confirmed by mutual understanding, the intimacy and extent of the relations and acquaintanceships among different co-operators, who confide their experience to each other, the settlement of weighty questions, like that of production, are among the most useful results of these congresses. Despite their usefulness, that distinguished gentleman, E. V. Neale, last October, proposed that congresses should be held every ten years only, because each congress costs, on an average, apart from the expense of stamps and postage, 239 *lire*. Up to the present, twenty-one congresses have been held; the first in

---

[1] In the last twenty-one congresses the chair was occupied, on the various days of sitting, on fifteen occasions by members of Parliament, five times by Professors (Rogers, Caird, Hodgson, Stuart, Marshall), twice by Bishops (Manchester and Durham); at other times by well-known men in politics and society, such as Lords Derby, Reay, the Marquis of Ripon, Hughes, Q. C., etc.

1869, at London, the last at Ipswich in 1889, which was inaugurated by Prof. Marshall of the University of Cambridge.

Before finishing this brief account I may be allowed to quote from a short work on pauperism by G. Howell, M.P., the following details with regard to the number of the poor in England from 1850 to 1889.

Years.	Number of Poor.	Proportion per 1000 inhabitants.
1849	1,088,569	62·7
1850-54	923,334	51·4
1855-59	894,822	47·0
1860-64	948,011	45·8
1865-69	926,075	44·9
1870-74	951,699	41·8
1875-79	752,977	30·9
1880-84	787,158	30·2
1885-89	788,357	28·3

From this table it appears that from 1849 to 1890 the number of poor has diminished by 300,000, and the proportion for every 1000 inhabitants is reduced to half. This view may be profitably compared with the table which shows the progress of co-operative societies. It cannot be said that the diminution in the number of poor depends solely on distributing co-operative societies, for certainly friendly societies, trades' unions, savings' banks, and other provident and benefit societies, have contributed to it, but it cannot be doubted that, however indeterminate, a relation, as of cause and effect, is evident in this comparison.

It is needless to recall how that the advantages, which have been briefly indicated, brought about in England by distributing societies, are due especially to the system adopted—that of selling at current prices to members and non-members, and dividing the profits among all the consumers in proportion to their consumption.

Germany.

In the autumn of 1852 there was established at Delitzsch among thirty-six fathers of families the first German distributing co-operative society, which to-day is of no great importance, and certainly has not, like the Rochdale Society in England, served as a model and example for other co-operative societies.

Although the most developed form of co-operation in Germany is that of credit, distributing societies which take the second place in respect of their development after that of credit, are sufficiently widespread, and a constant and rapid progress is observed in them, especially during the last few years. At the end of 1888 there were 760 German distributing societies; only in two years from 1886 to '88 their number had increased by 64.

The sale of goods takes place, as a rule, by ready-money payment, although it is still carried on to a great extent on credit, and at current prices. The net gain, after paying expenses and the interests on the capital, is distributed, part going to the reserve fund, part to the members as dividend. Through the new law which came in force the 1st October, 1889, sale is limited to members only; this law will be so far beneficial that it will lead to an increase in the number of members of those co-operative societies which before sold to non-members as well. However, this legislative restriction on the freedom of co-operative societies is certainly not praiseworthy or deserving of imitation.

Very many societies follow the "mixed" system of sale, *i.e.*, by means of a shop of their own, and by making contracts at the same time with other retail dealers in the case of those goods which they do distribute directly.

The constant progress of these societies may be seen in the number of societies which send their balance-sheet every year to the central office of the federation of German societies; and I take from the last published account of this office the following table showing the constant increase in the sales and the capital.

Year.	No. of Societies.	No. of Members.	Sales (Marks).	Joint-Capital (Marks).	Reserve (Marks).
1864	38	7,709	802,767	64,299	14,736
1865	34	6,647	925,383	66,678	8,301
1866	46	14,083	2,479,774	140,946	18,174
1867	49	18,884	2,903,922	216,558	33,480
1868	75	33,656	6,372,423	468,732	75,537
1869	109	42,286	7,126,251	626,151	122,571
1870	111	45,761	9,007,860	818,805	151,224
1871	143	64,517	13,522,974	1,589,571	221,526
1872	170	72,622	15,659,547	1,675,131	258,405
1873	189	87,504	21,882,408	2,414,127	353,064
1874	178	90,088	22,592,493	2,695,221	427,833
1875	179	98,055	22,704,963	2,912,265	503,409
1876	180	101,727	24,378,410	3,046,093	556,398
1877	202	99,862	26,503,379	3,199,532	671,319
1878	202	109,515	28,601,934	2,927,619	852,695
1879	191	130,777	28,772,988	3,204,677	954,723
1880	195	94,366	30,359,000	3,177,329	1,036,153
1881	185	116,510	32,761,636	3,088,788	1,206,289
1882	182	130,089	33,603,799	3,352,568	1,323,434
1883	172	110,433	32,684,302	3,052,519	1,477,673
1884	163	114,423	33,619,162	2,816,997	1,632,392
1885	162	120,150	25,136,555	3,319,098	1,735,746
1886	164	144,504	38,351,020	3,540,891	1,815,219
1887	171	154,460	41,441,685	3,691,784	1,953,616
1888	198	172,931	46,814,416	4,397,622	2,058,192

German distributing societies are not exclusively made up of workmen or country people. The following view, based on the data of 753 societies, shows the percentage of members in relation to the various classes of society.

Yeomen, gardeners, fishermen, rangers,   3·9 per cent.
Day labourers and workmen engaged in rural or
  forest occupations, in gardens and fishing,   3·5 ,,
Manufacturers, mine owners and architects,   1·2 ,,

Free (selbstständige) workmen,	15·2	per cent.
Free merchants and traders,	4·4	,,
Workmen attached to factories or mines,	42·9	,,
Ship-owners, hotel-keepers, brewers,	2·4	,,
Letter-carriers, railway servants, postal and telegraph clerks,	7·6	,,
Domestics,	1·7	,,
Doctors, apothecaries, teachers, artists, literary men, officers of Church and State,	9·0	,,
Rich persons, pensioners, and others without occupations	6·7	,,

German distributing societies owe their development in a large measure to the "general federation of German co-operative societies" (*Der allgemeine Verband der auf Selbsthülfe beruhenden deutschen Genossenschaften*) instituted by Schulze-Delitzsch for the object of "giving legal advice and replying to all the practical questions proposed." It is thus, so to speak, a psychical centre, but only a small proportion of the German societies belong to it (1150 out of 5950 which were in existence at the end of 1888). As intermediaries between this centre and the distributing societies, there are sub-federations, or provincial or district federations (*Unter-Provinzial* or *Landes-Verbände*), which look after the interests of the societies dependent on them and keep themselves *en rapport* with the central organ, prepare by means of special meetings for the annual general congress, for which deputies are chosen, and carry out the decisions of the congress. For the objects of the federation—exchanging notes of particular experiences, giving mutual advice and assistance, organising individual forces in order to obtain or preserve common advantages—are chiefly useful.

1st. As organ of the press, the *Blätter für Genossenschaftswesen* (formerly *Innung der Zukunft*), a journal "indispensable for every German society."

2nd. The German Social Bank of Sörgel Parrisius and Co., founded by Schulze in 1864, which had a capital, at the end of 1888, of 15 million marks.

The number of smaller federations dependent on the central federation were, in 1888, 34, 9 of them exclusively for distributing societies, *i.e.* :—

1st. That for the province of Brandenburg (seat, Berlin).

2nd. Silesia (seat, Breslau).

3rd. The province of Saxony and the adjacent provinces (seat, Magdeburg).

4th. Lausitz (seat, Görlitz).

5th. The Rhenish provinces and Westphalia (seat, Lüdenscheid).

6th. Saxony (seat, Chemnitz).

7th. Southern Germany (seat, Munich).

8th. Thuringia (seat, Jena).

9th. N. W. Germany (seat, Bremen).

If the psychical centre has considerably developed, there is still wanting in Germany an economical centre similar to the English "wholesales." An attempt was made to establish one at Mannheim; a

Waareneinkaufgesellschaft was formed among the societies of Southern Germany in the hope that the sphere of the central society might gradually extend to all the German distributing societies, but the attempt turned out premature, and, after some years, the society ceased to exist. But might it not have been easily foreseen that a central society at Mannheim, alone, for the whole of Germany was impossible? What saving of expense could there have been for Hamburg or Königsberg, for example, so far away from Mannheim?

Smaller agreements, however, were attempted between certain societies, even with success.

It was commenced by an interchange of information and opinions between adjacent societies with regard to commercial houses of which they had made trial. The centre of these exchanges of notices was established by sub-committees *(Unter-Verbände)* of distributing societies, who, with that object, issued appropriate circulars.

A federation of a few societies tried to put in circulation chests with samples *(Kasten mit Proben)* in order that the societies might be able to examine the quality of the goods for themselves; but this system was abandoned, because, during the circulation of these chests, which was naturally slow, the prices changed and the greater part of the societies could not depend upon them.

Later on, through agreement with wholesale traders who supplied the samples, there were instituted at Berlin goods' exchanges or exchange conferences (*Waarenbörsen* or *Börsenkonferenz*), which proved very serviceable, especially in the case of small societies. It is natural that an advantage should accrue to distributing societies from being able to compare, at the same moment, the different prices and qualities of the goods offered them by wholesale traders, whose competition is in this way much quickened. This advantage is felt still more sensibly by small societies who cannot have much knowledge or experience of wholesale trade; for their purchases in goods' exchanges small societies employ the manager of an important society, more able and competent than themselves, who, being on the spot, finds it no great trouble to buy for others.

Again, there are other distributing societies, doing a large trade, which act as wholesale societies for the smaller ones, as, for instance, the Breslau Society, for almost all the smaller societies of Silesia.

Two things, already specified by Schulze, are still to be desired in German distributing societies; the diminution of the very large number of societies which sell intoxicating liquors, and the abolition of sale on credit. If alcohol is often very useful in northern countries, one ought not therefore to favour its abuse; and that it *is* abused in Germany any one might be easily persuaded, even without seeing statistics, if he chanced to find himself in the provinces along the Rhine when the victory of the 3rd December is being celebrated.

France.

France, which has the glory and the fault of logic, in order to *emancipate* workmen, began with manufacturing co-operative societies. Some Frenchmen desire to boast the honour of having had a distributing society before the Rochdale, and with that view the Guebwiller is adduced, which existed in France so far back as 1832 under the name of *bread-bank*. Without entering into historical questions of no moment or of very doubtful utility, I observe that the Guebwiller Society was not a true co-operative society, because, while the joint capital was formed by the voluntary contributions of the work people of the firm of Schlumbert, their amount was estimated, in the case of each category of workmen, in proportion to their salary. This arrangement, admirable for the feeling of brotherly kindness displayed by the better paid workmen, violated, however, the co-operative principle, by which members, as such, must be equal.

There are now in France about 800 distributing co-operative societies, a third of which restrict themselves to the manufacture of bread, while the remainder sell eatables, boots and shoes, hats, stuffs, etc.

Co-operative shambles are rare; there are about 30 of them.[1]

The great majority sell goods charged with an amount varying from 10 to 12 per cent. above cost price; and the profits are distributed among the members in proportion to their consumption. The grave and very common fault is not to trouble about the increase of capital.

Many distributing co-operative societies are founded under the benevolent direction of *bourgeois*, that is to say, of large manufacturers, owners of mines, land, etc. Among these, for example, is the society founded thirty years ago by the *Compagnie d'Orléans* on the initiative of Cochin, and the Commentry Society, founded by M. Gibon, which, in August, 1888, had 483 members. The faults of these imperfect co-operative societies are—1st., the immediate lowering

---

[1] In the history of French distributing societies we have recorded the experiment made by Cernuschi at Paris in 1865. He spent 100,000 *lire* in order to prove that the distributing society cannot succeed and is "une pauvre formule." But the co-operative society founded by Cernuschi without assured custom, with a magnificent plant, a complicated system of accounts, a large expenditure for inspectors, controllers, cashiers, sub-cashiers, etc., and in order to carry on a butcher's shop—the most difficult form of distributing society—could it meet with good success? To these reasons let us add that Cernuschi's experiment had nothing co-operative about it, since all the capital was supplied by him, and then let any one say whether, seriously and dispassionately, the blame for this failure can be laid on the co-operative principle.

of the prices of articles, so that the workman increases his daily consumption, and afterwards finds himself in no better economic position than before; 2nd., not interesting the workman in the management of the business, not showing him at close quarters the mechanism and advantages of it.

Several societies adopt the English system. An interesting work of De Boyne,[1] published last year, allows of a short account being given of the pattern co-operative society of Nîmes. After a patient preparation, begun in the shape of a food society with philanthropic aims in 1859, there sprang up at Nîmes, in 1878, a distributing co-operative society on the system of ready-money payment at current prices, with distribution of dividends on consumption, and the formation of a reserve fund. At first, the members of the new store took turns in the service of sale. In 1879, a co-operative bake-house was founded. It is specially to be noticed that the women, warmly opposed to this society, because it obliged them to pay ready-money and purchase in the evening only, were reconciled to it after some months by the simple method of monthly meetings, where all their observations were discussed. In December, 1883, there was established at Nîmes a mutual-aid society, which, in 1884, formed an agreement with the distributing society with a view to a co-operative propaganda and

[1] *Histoire de la Coopération à Nîmes et son influence sur le mouvement coopératif en France*, Paris.

education. In April, 1886, the two societies were completely fused. To the Nîmes co-operators also belongs the credit of having founded, in 1886, a journal, *L'Emancipation*.

Many French societies are sufficiently prosperous: on this point, I extract some data from a little work shown at the last Paris exhibition :—[1]

Name of the Society.	Date of Balance Sheet.	No. of Members.	Capital.	Sales of the Year.	Net Profits.	Sums drawn from the profits for the provident or pension chest.
Mineur d'Anzin	28 Feb., 1888	3118	156,150	2,303,836	310,106	
Rendication Puteaux	31 Dec., 1888	1677	150,000	846,681	90,534	
Saint Remy-sur-Avre	31 Dec., 1888	1790	210,811	662,328	75,173	
Fraternellee de Cherbourg	31 Dec., 1888	1503	75,962	590,731	30,174	
Le xviii.e arrondissement Paris	31 Dec., 1888	1430	55,839	558,963	34,090	
Trith Saint Léger	31 Dec., 1888	1200	20,000	508,717	59,08;	11,608
Laborieuse Troyes	31 Dec., 1888	1445	40,900	436,904	38,788	
L'Egalitaire Paris	31 Dec., 1888	1400	—	425,362	17,326	
Agents P. L. M., Grenoble	31 Mar., 1889	560	34,465	375,824	11,11	
Employés P. L. M., Dijon	31 Mar., 1889	427	27,950	37,084	34,905	
L'Est à Mohon	30 Nov., 1888	414	41,373	310,208	17,348	
Union des Consommateurs	June, 1889	294	20,300	309,635	20,578	
PrévoyanceMontpelliéraine	31 Dec., 1888	873	43,700	270,555	13,587	15,857
Union ouvrière Lyon	31 Dec., 1888	623	57,291	265,000	8,500	6,793
Mines de Ferfay	2 Jan., 1889	550	12,500	209,345	19,73	
Alimentaire } Beaucourt }	9 Mar., 1889	558	53,980	258,209	18,074	
L'Est de Chaumont	31 Dec., 1888	587	30,000	246,831	23,746	
Choisy-le-Roi	31 Mar., 1889	872	46,575	208,582	3,752	
Agents P. L. M., Dôle	1 May, 1889	250	16,458	205,447	11,622	
L'Est de Neufchâteau	18 Mar., 1889	392	13,893	199,808	22,286	
Abeille Surenoise	31 Dec., 1888	698	114,800	193,780	20,900	
Soc. P. L. M., Villeneuve-S. Georges	12 Jan., 1889	430	20,387	179,373	9,820	
Soc. de Rethel	25 Dec., 1888	447	40,000	175,484	5,413	
Fraternelle de Lyon	31 Mar., 1889	549	27,450	152,76	6,098	
Prevoyance de Nimes	31 Dec., 1888	500	31,012	150,263	15,213	
Equitable co-opérateurs Lion	31 Dec., 1888	522	15,650	119,703	11,667	
Union fraternelle Voiron	31 Jan., 1889	1000	13,000	62,546	1,008	
Soc. du charbon Roubaix	31 Jan., 1889	238	11,900	62,404	13,570	

[1] *La question sociale réduite à une simple question de boutique*, Valenciennes, 1889.

For every 100 francs received from sales, 12·14 *lire* were distributed on an average, as net profits, among all the societies set down, and even 21·74 *lire* (*Roubaix*), which proves the good administration of these societies.

The average of net profits due to each member, in proportion to consumption, varies from 5 to 114 *lire*, with an average of about 60 *lire*.

It has been justly observed that co-operation in France has all the requisites for being a great force, but it is a scattered and unconscious force: it is a force which needs to be regulated, directed, organised. One difficulty in concentrating and directing these forces by common consent lies in the fact, brought out by Rostand, that the French are as timid in regard to economic progress, as they are rash and extravagant in other directions, and timidity facilitates no sort of progress.

The federation of French co-operative societies directed by Fougerousse and established in 1885, is, however, well organised, and now it is only sought to infuse more life into it by the formation of district centres which, in different nucleuses, may gather up the co-operative movement of various parts of France. In the third congress of French co-operators held at Tours in 1887 this very question was debated—the organising of fresh centres and the co-ordinating of those already in existence at Paris, Lyons, Tours, and

Nîmes. Political and personal questions, the very keen antagonism between the provinces and Paris, seriously obstructed this new organisation; but still an agreement was arrived at, and it was resolved that, besides the president and the general secretary residing at Paris, the federation should have as representatives in the country, in the individual centres, the district presidents, who were to meet at Paris at least once a year in order to discuss subjects of importance. Unluckily, however, this federation meets with strong opposition from the "syndicate of distributing societies," a union of about thirty associations, which is distinctly socialistic and almost revolutionary in character, while the federation does not meddle with politics and is not of a socialistic character.

As yet French societies have no central societies like the English "wholesales," but some years ago they established at Paris a kind of information agency. It placed itself *en rapport* with wholesale traders, inquired what abatements they were disposed to make on goods in given quantities, and published price lists: through its means the societies made contracts on far more advantageous terms than before, obtained larger discounts, and secured goods proceeding sometimes directly from producers. In 1886, in consequence of a vote of the Lyons Congress, there was established at Paris the first wholesale store for the northern district, which, in a few months, with a capital of only

8,000 francs, through the unwearied activity of Fougerousse did business to the amount of 150,000 francs. At Lyons and at Tours have been established two analogous district centres for the west and south of France. The different district centres, however, are entirely independent: the Paris centre is an association formed like the English "wholesales," and differs from them only in this, that it sells to the societies at a little higher than the cost prices, the ultimate gains, however, being always divided in proportion to the purchases.

Italy.

Distributing societies, although after popular banks they represent the most wide-spread form of co-operation among us, have not yet attained any great development or importance. Generally, the multiplicity of small dealers who are satisfied with scanty gains and sell many articles, the sobriety of the population, especially in the south, the small need of firing and the mildness of the current retail prices for a long time caused the need of these societies to be less felt than elsewhere. Now that the mildness of prices is only a tender memory, the need of these societies is felt more strongly; and if it had not been for the famous Art. 5 of the law of 1870, if the prolific Rochdale system, advertised and commended by Buffoli and Rabbeno, had been better known, especially to the numerous mutual aid societies,[1] Italian distributing societies would have been stronger and more numerous.

Now the new movement, formed on the pure English system, initiated at Sampierduna, and confirmed with wonderful results by the *Unione Cooperativa* of Milan, commences to spread at Turin, Rome, Naples, and in other smaller centres of population, giving good promise of the future.

The first distributing store arose at Turin, being promoted by the powerful working-men's mutual aid association, founded in 1850. Data are wanting to

[1] Mutual aid societies are the school in which distributing societies were prepared. In England, writes Ludlow, the humdrum mutual aid society prepared our working classes for social self-government, and formed the spirit of independence and association. Signor Ferri said, at the third congress of Italian co-operators, that these societies have become dry leaves in the great tree of popular providence, and can be verified only by direct contact with the true oxygen, which is co-operation. Certainly all provident institutions are very far from being of the same value to the workman as return to work when he is idle, and economy and saving when he is busy, but it is only right to observe that these dry leaves are not to be despised, and only a small proportion of elect can arrive at the heights of co-operation without passing through smaller experiments of reciprocity. In fortifying mutual aid, the chief moral and material substance of the people is fortified, and prepared for greater undertakings—this is the primary school of providence and is indispensable for mounting to the higher grades.

show the progress of the co-operative idea among us, which, however, has been especially accentuated during the last five years. It was only in 1885 that official researches were commenced to investigate into the co-operative institutions annexed to mutual aid societies. The data supplied by Fano in 1869 and those collected in 1873 by a Government sub-commission for provident and labour institutes, composed of Signori Ellena, Fano and Romanelli, are still uncertain. More recent and reliable data are found in the reports of Italian co-operative societies, but the latest and most exact notices are those collected by the Minister of Agriculture, Industry, and Commerce, consequent on a circular to the prefects the 5th March, 1889, N. 349.

The administrators of our societies showed a general reluctance to furnish the data requested, and many of the forms drawn up by Signor Bodio perished in the waste-paper baskets of the societies. This hindrance to a complete set of statistics is partly founded, as Maffi well observes, on an innate distrust in our unions which it is difficult to conquer or destroy: they fear lest the notices asked for should have no other object but furnishing the Government with data for the imposition of some additional tax.

Here, in any case, are the data presented by the recent Bodio report in consequence of the circular referred to.

In the catalogue are registered 683 stores, 187 of them legally constituted, 267 real societies and 189 annexed to mutual aid societies. In these numbers are included 35 co-operative bake-houses. Some other societies work a mill: but both the bake-house and the mill are on the capitalist model, *i.e.*, by means of paid workmen: so that they could in no case be placed among manufacturing co-operative societies. The stores which sent details scarcely amount to a third of those of which there are notices.

The capital of independent distributing societies (whether legally constituted or not) is nearly always formed by means of shares payable in instalments, the value of which varies from 5 to 100 *lire*. The capital of stores annexed to mutual aid societies, in the majority of cases, is formed on the contrary by drawing on the estate of the societies themselves, a system which is evidently very dangerous.

The most important stores sell to the public. Of 153 societies, of which there are more detailed notices, 16 sell at current prices, the rest at cost price, holding this necessary in order to attract members and purchasers. Of 120 stores, 66 sell for cash only, and 54 also on credit. Among these 54 there are several stores formed by railway officials, in which case sales on credit are less dangerous.[1] In general the gross

---

[1] On the *Unione Militare* which, however, grants a limited

profit on the shares varies from 8·2 to 12·6 per cent.: the net profit from 2·3 to 3·5: the net profit on the capital from 13 to 16 per cent. How much progress has still to be made before we can have a net profit, calculated on the capital, from 50 to 100 per cent., as on an average English societies have.[1]

The question is being still agitated among us respecting the advisability of forming a central co-operative society similar to English "wholesales;" though it is recognised that for the present there exist almost insuperable obstacles. The inertia of many of our co-operative societies, the absence of relations and acquaintanceship between them, the scarcity of means, due especially to the system of sale, the great diversity in their constitution, and the topographical arrangement of Italy, on account of which societies, scattered through districts very remote from each other and having different needs, can with difficulty be grouped round a common centre, are the chief obstacles to forming a "wholesale."

credit, see *La cooperazione nell 'esercito e nella marina* printed at Rome by the tipografia Aldina, 1888, and an article by Captain F. D. Chaurand in the *Revista militare* of November, 1889. In these writings there are fitting studies of the English *Army and Navy* and the *Deutschen Offizier Verein*, instituted at Berlin in 1881, and the precise reasons are explained why the *Unione* has not been modelled exclusively either on the one or the other of these societies.

[1] *La co-operazione italiana*, July, 1889.

From a comparison made by Buffoli between the distances from Milan to the Italian towns where are our best-known co-operative societies, and that from Manchester to the towns where the most important co-operative societies which existed previous to 1863 have their seat, it follows that on an average the English societies were 83 kilomètres distant from the central co-operative society, while the Italian would be 270.

Although no economic progress can transform the topographical arrangement of Italy, it is not right therefore to abandon the hope of establishing a central society.

There is nothing to prevent a city more central than Milan being chosen as the seat of the society and branch establishments being opened as in England: nor can it be extravagant to hope that the railway companies would grant special reductions for the transport of goods, as is already done in the case of some commercial firms, like Cirio & Co., or that cheap transport should render the distances almost a matter of indifference.[1]

Much graver for the moment are the other obstacles

---

[1] In Texas, which exhibits an immense length and breadth of about 10·0 kilomètres, there exists a central society with its seat at Galveston. So too in the United States the pigs of Iowa are despatched to Chicago to be butchered, and are then sent back to Iowa to be eaten.

referred to, insomuch that if a single central store were established, either it could not work or it would fail. On these grounds Italian co-operators resigned for the moment the idea of a single economic centre, instead whereof it was proposed to form district stores in imitation of France: but these also are not without difficulties.

Buffoli, *à propos* of this, in the article cited, justly observes: "Different and special stores would be needed, *i.e.*, one at Naples for southern wine and pastry: one at Bologna for salt meat: one at Genoa for colonial produce, oil, and pastry: one at Milan for cheese and butter: one at Turin for Piedmont wine, etc. But before these district stores could have a consumption sufficient to cover expenses and procure at the same time a saving for the societies which applied to them for purchases, evidently the number and power of the societies themselves must greatly increase—a thing which in common with all co-operators I warmly desire."

In some districts, however, it is not the number which is deficient for the purpose of establishing these stores, but especially and always the fault is lack of means, due to sale at cost price and the inertia of many societies. Indeed, from an analysis published by the *Credito e Cooperazione*, 15th March, 1890, compiled on the strength of recent investigations with the assistance of the General Direction of Statistics, the distribution on the 31st November, 1889, is found to have been as follows:—

	Societies legally constituted.	Independent Societies not legally constituted.	Societies annexed to Mutual Aid Societies
Piedmont,	40	91	192
Liguria,	13	11	4
Lombardy,	28	40	14
Venetia,	10	15	12
Emilia,	10	15	10
Umbria,	9		5
Marche,	4	1	3
Tuscany,	42	20	16
Rome,	3	—	2
Abruzzi and Molise,	1	—	—
Campania,	6	2	8
Apulia,	2	6	5
Calabria,	2	—	3
Basilicata,	1	—	2
Sicilia,	8	2	12
Sardinia,	1	—	—
	180	203	288

Grand Total, 671.

And who can say that in Piedmont, for example, where there are altogether 323 distributing societies, and little Liguria and Lombardy, there is not a sufficient number of societies to maintain a central district store? It is not number which is wanting, but concord, energy, means. A painful, but salutary, warning was given recently at Vercelli, where a central store had been set up for providing thirty-four adjacent societies with articles of consumption. In 1887 the system of supplies, by means of leases, was used in Vercelli by these societies, and it was only

K

later that the central store was established, the result of which was awaited with lively interest (Remussi Report to the Congress of 1888); but, as Signor Carotti assures me, the experiment is a miserable failure.[1]

[1] During the printing of these sheets the information reaches us that at Turin, on the 10th December this year, a wholesale distributing co-operative society was established with a savings-bank or annuity fund. From the *Gazetta Piedmontese* (Nos. 254 and 255) we take the following data : " The wholesale society is composed of charitable institutions and distributing co-operative societies: to charitable institutions it promises important savings on the purchase prices, thus increasing their opportunities of doing good :. to co-operative societies it secures a considerable reduction in the distributing prices. We are sorry that we cannot obtain more minute particulars as to this co-operative society."

With regard to the savings-bank, Signor S. Regis, the inventor of this form of co-operation, read the statute at the meeting of the 10th. " We learn from this that each member would form an annuity, not by direct sacrifices, but simply by providing himself with all the articles he requires at the co-operative stores, whose profits, resulting from the sale of goods, purged from the expenses of administration and from the dividend on the shares, and computed at their actual value, will, through the agency of the Council of Administration, be paid to the special savings-bank. The functions of this savings-bank would be : 1st, to obtain yearly from the co-operative association the certified amount of the stores' annual profits, and to enter these profits to the single account of each member in proportion to the amount of his purchases ascertained from the several certificates ; 2nd, to liquidate the annuity at 45 years of age, and only 15 of seniority on the basis of a return of the capital saved, or to liquidate and refund, on the member's demand, the amount of his savings ; to refund the capital saved,

But if district centres are not yet practicable, could not the best societies of great cities, like Turin, Milan, Florence, Bologna, group together the various distributing co-operative societies scattered up and down the country, and act for these smaller societies as central societies, just as the Breslau society does for those of Silesia? Besides the economic advantages which would be obtained, by eliminating a greater number of intermediaries, they would multiply the relations between the various societies, and through mutual knowledge and confidence it would be possible to prepare the societies for more complex and useful organisations: moreover, there would be the advantages derived from intimate relations with, and the prolific abiding examples of, societies of the Rochdale type, to spread a conviction of the usefulness of this system, and to induce many co-operative societies to conform to it, so as to make all the societies of a uniform organisation, which would facilitate still more the establishment of central societies.

The psychical centre, to use Rabbeno's phrase, on the other hand, is very easily organised among us.

At the first congress of Italian co-operators, held at Milan in 1886, a report was presented *on the advis-*

either before or after compliance with the conditions for the liquidation above mentioned, to the family or heirs by will of the deceased member." Our best wishes for this new institution.

ability and on the methods of a federation of Italian co-operative societies; and in the second congress of 1887, Prof. U. Gobbi presented the sketch of a statute for the federation of Italian co-operative societies, which, with very slight modifications, was approved, "with the object of promoting the development of co-operative unions and their co-ordination."

For this federation a central committee of co-operative societies was appointed, whose duties were indicated in a general way, without entering into particulars, and reference was only made in a special way to the periodical, *La cooperazione italiana,* which is to publish: 1st, the acts of the central committee and of co-operative societies; 2nd, notes on Italian and foreign co-operative societies; 3rd, information of interest to co-operative societies, signed articles, etc.

One cannot, even in a summary and incomplete account of Italian distributing societies, neglect to mention the importance of three Italian congresses, in which, putting aside all political differences, practical co-operators and men of distinction in politics and science discuss co-operation. The usefulness of these congresses is not immediate, nor can it be estimated arithmetically; but, certainly, the interchange of ideas and experience, the concord and the impetus given to the societies by the decisions taken, and the propaganda in the newspapers increasingly facilitate the spread of sound co-operative principles. We heartily wish that the fourth congress, which is being held on the 5th of October, this year, at Turin, and in which very important questions are to be discussed with respect to co-operation, may be, no less than the others, fruitful in useful lessons.

Our movement is powerfully supported also by the press; besides *La cooperazione italiana* (Milan), the *Bolletino della cooperazione italiana* (Caserta), *Credito e cooperazione* (Rome), *La cooperazione rurale* (Padua), *Il bolletino della associazione generale degli operai braccianti di Ravenna*, which are exclusively taken up with co-operation, many Italian newspapers and even our best reviews contribute to the propagation of co-operative principles. But even in the propaganda by means of the press would it not be desirable that we too should have a single journal like the *Co-operative News*, which should be the organ of Italian co-operative societies, and teach sound principles? Our geographical conditions which, even in the sphere of politics, prevent non-official journals having that general circulation which they enjoy in England, are an obstacle also to this special form of unification. But could not Italian co-operators who, from the very fact of their being such, already show a high moral and intellectual education, cast off these close fetters and agree to found a single newspaper?

Switzerland.

The distributing societies of Switzerland have sprung up very slowly; their origin dates back to 1852.

The first attempt to compile statistics of these societies was made in 1883; from the quasi-compulsory entry of the associations in the "trade register," it was possible to verify the existence of 123 distributing societies divided among 19 cantons or semi-cantons, and doing business, according to an approximate valuation, to the extent of about 13 million francs per annum. In 1887, there were 142 of these societies, and only four cantons were still unprovided with them. Now, the Helvetic societies amount to 160, a considerable number compared with the small Swiss population, but which does not indicate any very great importance owing to the fewness of the members and the small amount of business of many of these societies, which, for the most part, are very far from practising co-operation according to the Rochdale system.

The Helvetic societies devote themselves almost exclusively to the sale of articles of food, especially of bread; a small number of them keep as accessories clothes, boots, and shoes, etc. Their members are, for the most part, working-people; but in cities like Zurich, Basle, Geneva, Lausanne, the well-to-do class supplies numerous members, and generally also administrators.

In January this year the Helvetic distributing societies met at Olten, and deliberated about the founding of a *Swiss Union of Distributing Societies*. Up to the present thirty-seven societies have given in their adhesion to it, and no question is felt but that this number must increase rapidly. The presidency was entrusted to the Basle Society, perhaps the best administered and most prosperous in all Switzerland. The object of the new league is contained in the first article of its statute.

The Union proposes as its object the protection and development, from an economic point of view, of the interests of the societies affiliated to it, as also the collective protection of these interests at home and abroad. It secures the attainment of this object by organising the interchange of experience among the united societies, by collecting and classifying statistical data, by giving advice and useful information to the societies, by diffusing the true principles on which the association must practically repose, by procuring notices on the quality and sources of wares and other objects necessary for existence ; in a word, by keeping *au courant* of all that may interest either the Union or any society taken separately.

The organs of the association are, 1st., the assembly of delegates ; 2nd., the directing committee.

The societies whose effective does not exceed 300 members have a right to one delegate to the assembly, those numbering from 500 to 1000 members have a right to two delegates, those numbering over a thousand have a right to three. The assembly of delegates appoints every year the society to whom the direction belongs, and it is the administrators of this who elect the five members of the directing committee.

The position of presiding society may be assigned for several years following to the same society, if the assembly thinks this convenient. The same may be said of the members of the directing committee, who are always eligible for re-election. It rests with the committee to decide whether or not it is expedient to admit societies to the Union after an examination of their statutes, and most recent accounts. But a society, once admitted, cannot be excluded except by a resolution of the assembly of delegates. The central bank is fed by contributions of the societies, which vary from 12 to 60 *lire* a year, according to the number of the members of each association.

The first two points with which the Union is now dealing are: on the one hand, the elaboration of statistics of Swiss co-operation; on the other, preparation for collective action in the Federal Chambers, in order to resist every new increase in the import duties on the necessaries of life.

Belgium.

The first Belgian distributing society was established in 1865 at Liège, but there was no considerable co-operative movement till within the last four or five years. There are now 150.

One division of them is occupied solely with the manufacture or sale of bread and flour, a very few, and those unsuccessfully, of meat, and some with the sale of different articles of food, as also coal, boots and shoes, clothes, drapery, medicine. Some societies agree with merchants in order to obtain reductions on those articles which they do not sell. Societies among officials sometimes propose to secure easy credit for their members and build houses; those among working-men, and they are the most numerous, have insurance banks attached, and pursue different objects for the protection of the working class.

Part of the societies, like the *Vooruit*, sell to members only: some to the workmen of a single factory, but many others to the public as well. The amount of the capital and the value of the shares vary according to the societies: often the shares are of very small dimensions, and do not afford interest; manifold are the societies inspired by socialistic ideas.[1] They

[1] *Het socialismus voert de beschaving tot haar toppunt* (socialism brings civilisation to its perfection), is one of the mottoes inscribed on the walls of the *Vooruit.*

generally sell at a mild price, and divide the profits in proportion to the consumption : some, however, sell at the lowest price, and others make over the profits to the shares : not seldom part of the profits is set apart for socialistic or prudential uses. Rarely, however, do these societies promote saving : and instead of capitalising the profits assigned on consumption, they commonly distribute them without more ceremony : oftenest in bonds for the purchase of goods.

These associations have encountered strong opposition : in several cities merchants have combined against them, attacking them in all sorts of ways; have formed themselves into an anti-co-operative league in order to exert influence in elections, choosing deputies opposed to co-operation : they have especially made war on officials, disputing their right to meddle with matters outside their office, and appealing in vain to the Government to stop them ; and finally they have attempted even to "boycot" co-operators, by agreeing not to give work either to them or their families. The principal cause of this opposition is the purely socialistic tendency given to very many co-operative societies, which has aroused against them all the hatred occasioned by political passion : insomuch that several societies, in order to avoid this contest, have publicly announced that politics are altogether excluded from the society.[1]

[1] *De politiek is strengelijk uitgesloten*, is among the funda-

A special feature in Belgium is the popular dispensaries: they were begun in the first place at Brussels, and were afterwards introduced at Verviers, Liège, Ghent, and Anvers. Those at Brussels, founded in 1882 by a federation of mutual-aid societies, which established a co-operative society for the purpose, are actually six in number: the society which administers them is composed of 75 federated societies, having altogether about 10,000 members. In 1888 it had a capital of 21,000 francs, a reserve of 60,000 francs, and although it sold at moderate prices, it had reached the comparatively enormous figure of 54,340 francs' profits, half of which went to the reserve for the institution of new dispensaries, and to the total of the social fund, and half to the shareholding societies in proportion to the aggregate scales.

An association which deserves special mention is the *Vooruit* of Ghent. The *Vooruit* (which in Flemish signifies *forwards*), promoted by the Socialist party, is the centre for the spread of socialistic ideas, and derives from co-operation the material forces for animating many different projects.

It was founded in 1883 with a fund of 2000 francs, borrowed from the syndical chamber of the Ghent weavers: its basis is a great co-operative society. Its socialistic character is shown by the way in which

mental principles of the *Volksbelang*, which has 5000 members, and of other societies.

the capital is formed: the members, who are now about 4000, contribute to it but little, by the payment of 50 *centesimi* as entrance fee, and by foregoing a single *lira* of the profits due to them on consumption: the true capital is formed from the reserve, and is therefore collective.

The *Vooruit* has nine branches: its principal business is the manufacture of bread, the profits on which it returns to members in proportion to consumption; the price of bread is 35 *centesimi* the kilogram—the average of the current prices of bread at Ghent—12 of which are afterwards returned to the purchaser: it sells also coal, stuffs, boots and shoes, groceries and drugs. It does not promote the capitalisation of the savings, and this is undoubtedly the greatest defect of these societies, being closely connected with the socialistic character of the institution. The quotas of profits are returned in the following way: if, for instance, a member has purchased to the amount of 200 kilograms of bread at 35 *centesimi*, and if the half-yearly balance-sheet shows that the cost of each kilogram was only 23 *centesimi*, that member will have a saving of (200 × 12) 24 francs, which the administration changes into so many purchase bonds.

Denmark.

Distributing societies were introduced there in 1860

on the English pattern, but the co-operative movement acquired vigour only in the years subsequent to 1870, and yielded the best results. In 1885 there existed from 180 to 200 societies with more than 20,000 members, and with a capital of 500,000 *krone*.

In January, 1886, at Copenhagen, a large society was established for purchasing goods wholesale, in order to supply them to the particular associations which form part of it, and with the object also of carrying on a propaganda in favour of co-operation, and putting itself *en rapport* with the co-operative societies of other countries.

Sweden and Norway.

In Sweden the imitation and development of the co-operative movement are specially due to a rich and benevolent manufacturer, Mr. Oscar Smith. A few years ago, through his means, in the villages of Sweden there began to be established distributing societies which are now, it seems, being successfully propagated. Afterwards, in 1883, Smith founded at Stockholm co-operative kitchens, by means of a special organisation, *working men's circles* or *rings* (*Sättskapet Arbetarnes Rings*). Of these circles there are now at Stockholm 24, associated one with the other, and they have (at the close of '89) a total of 24,600 members; each of them has a kitchen in which participation in the profits is arranged for in proportion to consumption. The institution of these circles has been followed by such good results that, in less than two years, more than 80 of them sprang up in the Swedish provinces.

With regard to Norway I have less recent notices. Doctor Bloch wrote in 1884: "In Norway also there are distributing societies, but they have made but little way; for retail trade is usually so well organised that there is less need felt of them than elsewhere. Moreover distributing societies have not always prospered, because they do not work by ready money payment in the purchases and sales—a necessary principle, if these associations are to succeed."

Holland.

Distributing societies are not unknown in Holland either. Under the title of *Nederlandsche Coöperative Band* there has been established this year at the Hague the central association of Dutch co-operative societies, as a distinct branch of the meritorious *Eigen Hulp*, which has already actively promoted co-operative principles in the kingdom.

The central association has been founded by 14 distributing stores at Amsterdam, Arnheim, Bergen, Delft, the Hague, Haarlem, Helder, Herzogenbosch, Leuwarden, Leida, Nieuwegen, Rotterdam, Utrecht and

Vlissingen. The society is divided into two sections,— the commercial section which provides for wholesale purchases: the administrative which has as its object the propaganda, diffusion, and legal ordering of co-operation.

Austria—Hungary.

The most important districts with regard to the spread of distributing co-operative societies are Bohemia, Moravia, Upper and Lower Austria, the Tyrol, Voralberg, and Styria. On the 31st December, 1889, there existed in Austria 236 distributing societies, and 51 in Hungary. The sale of these societies is limited, as a rule, to articles of food and firing; many sell at cost prices, and credit is subjected to great abuse. If to these obstacles we add the lack of good administrators, the invasion of politics into the sphere of co-operation, the indifference of most people, and the oppressiveness of certain imposts, it may be easily understood why these societies have made little progress. *Die Genossenschaft* is an important organ of co-operative societies.

United States.

The first attempts to establish distributing societies were made in 1831 in Massachusetts, but they had little of a co-operative character about them. These associations have not yet acquired the same importance in the United States as in England; the causes of this diversity in the development of the same institution in two peoples so nearly related as these, are clearly summed up by Rabbeno. The general prosperity of the country, the good economic position in which, thanks to high wages, the working-men are found, and the vast development of trade in articles of consumption, whose prices, owing to the great competition, are considerably reduced, cause the need of these expedients to be more seldom felt than in Europe. Besides the need being less felt, frequent failures helped to diminish the importance of these societies. Warner, who deals especially, as he says, with the pathology of co-operation, enumerates among the causes of failure, deficiency of capital, the want of suitable legislation, such as to allow the formation of true co-operative societies, the general habit of selling on credit, the hostility of traders, which was all the stronger on account of the bold announcement of a wish to abolish all "middlemen." Further, bad organisation, which easily changed these co-operative into speculative societies, the frequent robberies of administrators, the almost total absence of persons devoting themselves to them, as in Europe, from a philanthropic motive, and also, as Walker observes, the indifference of the people to small savings, have greatly hampered the spread of these unions. Besides, in the great American cities the consumer is almost in direct contact with the producer; thus at New York brewers have their own shops and sell retail in different parts of the city by means of suitable paid managers. In this case a distributing co-operative society has very little to save, because there is no intermediary to replace.

Nevertheless, the distributing societies of the United States deserve notice on account of the activity which they have displayed during the last few years.

It is necessary to distinguish, in this country, the movement carried on by certain great organisations spread all over the United States, and the sporadic movement of associations which sprang up here and there by means of different initiatives. Sometimes the efforts of independent co-operative societies reduced themselves to meeting "commissions" among the members of the local "grange" (the "grange" is a section or branch of the great association of the "Patrons of Industry"); for some time this was recognised to be useful, but when a delay arose in the delivery of the goods, or these were not altogether satisfactory, and especially when it was found inconvenient to pay ready-money, the system of commissions began to be abandoned, and thus many societies gradually came to an end.

The first important co-operative movement is that

from 1845 to 1860, the second begins after 1870, when the great economic crisis, the general economic distress, followed by the War of Secession, caused the need of association and economy to be felt in various classes.

The movement was chiefly promoted by two grand organisations, that of the "Patrons of Husbandry" (which arose in 1867), and that of the "Sovereigns of Industry" (which arose in 1874), the sections of which ("granges" or "councils") were rapidly multiplied. In 1880, the rage for these societies having ceased with the improvement in the economic conditions of the country, the dissolution of these organisations was completed. It is only later that distributing societies have sprung up, and now they show signs of reorganisation on a vast scale.

I have already indicated how the Rochdale system was introduced, and what excellent fruits it bore in the United States; among the best of these societies I mention only the *Hartington Co-operative Association* in Indiana, founded in 1880, and the *Laramie Co-operative Association*, which, at the end of 1887, had a capital of 7,820 dollars. There is an important house of commissions at Baltimore, *The Maryland Grange Agency*, founded in 1876, which does business at the rate of from 300,000 to 500,000 dollars per annum, and having paid expenses and a moderate interest on the capital, gives back about 9,000 dollars in proportion to the purchases,

The advantages which, in the United States, are recognised as flowing from the spread of co-operative stores (*stores* correspond to the English *shop*) are educational, through their having made known the benefits of association, and hygienic (many co-operative societies have resolved not to sell intoxicating liquors), and they have also helped to combat certain coalitions and to habituate people to go direct to producers.

A true and real central society for purchases and sales wholesale does not exist in the United States. The " wholesale " founded at Cincinnati in 1880, between the societies of Ohio, Indiana, Kentucky, and West Virginia, had in 1886 to liquidate, owing to the general apathy of the members, want of capital and bad administration.

Now, the idea of co-operation goes on increasing in popularity, and herein the powerful association of the *Knights of Labour*, which has adopted the principle first proclaimed by the *Knights* of Chicago ("down with the strike fund and up with the co-operative fund"), and which has as its object, to promote a universal co-operative system, is of great assistance. By means of these knights there was founded in 1886, in Ohio, the *American Coöperative Union*, which seems to have had quite a local origin, but aims " at combining in a great union all provident and benefit institutions, trades' unions, religious and co-operative associations of every kind, and every other society or union of whatever nature or name designed to carry the advantages of co-operation among the intricate interests of all." From the report presented at the Paris Congress, it appears that 51 distributing societies sprang up in the order of the *Knights of Labour*. According to the statistics published in 1889, there exist 270 distributing societies in the United States, the greater number (155) of them in Texas. Owing to the impetus given by the *Knights of Labour* and the diffusion of the good results of the Rochdale system, the American co-operative movement is constantly acquiring new strength, and the first congress of American co-operators was held this year at Chicago.

In conclusion, a phrase of Luzzati may be commended to some of these distributing stores, which, as Warner relates, hold their meetings with precautions against conspirators, and wrap all information concerning them in the profoundest mystery, and that is that "in a co-operative society nothing must be hidden, nothing attenuated. It must resemble a solid and transparent palace; everyone ought to look into it without difficulty. In every point it should reflect fidelity, uprightness, honour."

Co-operation is not unknown in South America: at Buenos Ayres, there has existed, ever since 1878, a distributing society, *Sociedad cooperativa de Almacenas limitada,* which, in 1887, had about 700 members, and sold to the extent of about 50,000 *lire* per month; its object is to reduce prices, and, above all, to check adulterations of goods, which, at Buenos Ayres, have taken enormous proportions.

At Melbourne also, in Australia, there are two distributing co-operative societies, which, however, so far, have not yielded results of much importance; it would appear that in these new rich countries, where wages run very high, the petty economies which co-operation is able to effect on consumption are but slightly appreciated by working-men.

In Africa, too, there is the *Co-operative Society, Limited,* founded in 1886 at Alexandria in Egypt. Its first statement of accounts from May to December, 1886, is tolerably satisfactory; at the end of the year the members were 218, and the shares subscribed—a pound each—1810.

I observe, in conclusion, that one cannot, as some have maintained, call the Russian *artel,* or artisans' associations, distributing societies: these are societies more in name than in fact, and the word "save" is almost entirely unknown to the Russian labourer—spendthrifty, careless of the morrow, who drinks or gambles away as much as he earns. Distributing societies, if practicable, would be of great service in Russia, where in almost every city there exists a central benevolent committee, to which all the other sectional committees (*uciastky, otdielenija*) apply. These latter, usually, are instituted by the most influential ladies, with the assistance of a few notables, who might usefully promote co-operative societies.

CHAPTER VII.

RELATIONS BETWEEN DISTRIBUTING AND MANUFACTURING CO-OPERATIVE SOCIETIES.

ACCORDING to the view of very many co-operators, distributing societies, in order to be a cause of the general amelioration and progress of the working classes, ought to give rise to manufacturing co-operative societies, thanks to the capital gradually accumulated by small savings on consumption. Generally, distributing societies have assigned to them the task of habituating people to association and forming a capital in order to give rise to more difficult and complex forms of co-operation, for, if it almost suffices for the existence of distributing societies that there should be consumers, other forms of co-operation cannot be originated without capital.

In practice this ideal is attained, when, indeed, it *is* attained, very slowly; but more frequently it is the custom to make the two aforesaid phases of providence, education, or wholesale central societies precede. In France and Italy the institution of provident banks, mutual life assurances, annuities' banks,[1] etc., is considered the best employment of the funds collected by distributing societies. In England, on the contrary, the first two phases have been already passed, and now the transition is being prepared to manufacturing co-operative societies.

An objection has been urged against these provident and mutual assurance institutions, springing from distributing societies, on the ground that they divert the capital from its true objective:

"*La retraite est une bonne chose, mais chaque chose doit venir en son temps, et sera seulement quand la co-opération aura organisé la production qu'elle pourra prélever sur les profits de cette production de quoi assurer une retraite aux ouvriers qu'elle emploie.* To secure bread for one's old age is a selfish action, while the object of co-operation is to work,

[1] At Lyons the co-operative bakehouse allots about a centime for every kilogram of bread to an annuities' bank for members in old age.

At Vienna, also, 40 per cent. is drawn from the net gains for a bank for old age.

The *Unione Cooperativa* of Milan presents an example of the same thing in the interest of its servants; considering it their duty to provide for extraordinary accidents to their servants, and at the same time to accustom them to economy and prudence, it founded a "provident bank," to which is assigned—1st, 5 per cent. of the nett savings as shown by the balance sheet; 2nd, the fines inflicted on the *personnel*; 3rd, a monthly withdrawal of 2 per cent. from the fixed salaries of each servant; 4th, the interest on the bank fund.

certainly for oneself, but also and above all for others; and I believe that the true office of co-operation is to aim at collective advantages, and that it is lowering its value to make it subserve individualist objects."[1]

To me the institution of these provident funds does not appear, strictly, an offence against the co-operative principle. Why should distributing societies employ their capital in enterprises which are still very risky, like manufacturing societies, which in all countries and at all times have so far met with very scant success? The able Fougerousse justly observed, at the Tours Congress, that capital employed in manufacturing co-operative societies is still too much involved in risk, and warmly commending provident institutions, concluded: "*Il faut savoir marché* (sic) *par étapes et ne pas pretendre, du premier coup, conquérir le monde et faire l'assaut de sommets.*" Blessings ought to be carried where they are most needed, and where their usefulness is most certain: providence is not difficult to apply, and co-operative institutions ought to revive and enlarge the pure and perennial sources of mutual aid, which raised the first hospital tent, whither the phalanxes of our afflicted

---

[1] Gide, *De la coopération et des transformations qu'elle est appelée à realiser dans l'ordre economique.* (Speech made at Paris at the International Congress of Distributing Societies, 8th September, 1889.) *Revue d'économie politique*, n. 5, 1889.

toilers, with less uncertainty as to the future, still repair.

As against the ideal of the harmony of the various forms of co-operation, set forth by Gide and by many co-operators, *i.e.*, that of arriving sooner or later, by means of distributing societies, at manufacturing societies, we may set an observation implied in the definition of "society" given by Proudhon, *i.e.*, "an aggregation of which it may always be said that the members, being united for themselves only, are united against the world."

The numerous data collected by Rabbeno in his study of manufacturing co-operative societies—the best monograph on this subject extant—seem to justify Proudhon rather than the others. In point of fact, he writes, the distributing society is co-operative in so far as consumers unite in order to carry on, and for themselves alone, the work of distribution; the credit society is co-operative in so far as those in need of credit unite in order to perform for themselves, and themselves alone, the task of supplying credit; the building society is co-operative in so far as those in need of houses unite in order to provide themselves with such houses as are suitable for them; the manufacturing society is co-operative in so far as those who need to take up manufacture—*i.e.*, have need of the enterprise, take it up in common. Theoretically, therefore, there is a manifest conflict of interest between distributing and manufacturing societies. While distributing societies aim at purchasing goods at the lowest possible prices in order to obtain a great saving in the distribution, manufacturing societies are interested in selling at the highest prices in order to distribute to their members a large quota of profits, and, therefore, any agreement will be impossible, for it will not be right for distributing societies to make their purchases from manufacturing co-operative societies in preference to other producers, who may sell to them on better terms.

The English instance, adduced by Rabbeno, seems to confirm this antagonism in practice. In England many societies employed capital by devoting themselves directly to production. First arose, in 1854, the *Rochdale Manufacturing Co-operative Society*, a bold attempt which was followed by the best results; then other societies were established, and among the first, in order of time, the *Oldham Sun Mill Company*. The " wholesales " also applied themselves directly to the manufacture of those goods which they more especially required; and many societies, united in " federations," devoted themselves to the manufacture of those products which the " wholesales " did not supply on sufficiently favourable terms.

But, writes Rabbeno again, if the manufacturing enterprise is based on consumption, if, that is to say, it is worked directly by consumers with the object, not of speculating, but of obtaining a larger saving on their purchases, the predominance will naturally fall to the consumption element, which, in its turn, will act the lion's part, keeping all the advantages for itself and giving as little as possible to labour and capital. And it will be a fact that a business begun without any speculative aim, will end by having one, and will directly rob the elements of production which have also a right to their share. Unless it be that capital necessarily assumes much importance in the enterprise, and that it belongs either to a great extent or altogether to the "speculator consumers"; in which case a certain compromise will follow between the interests of the speculators as consumers and as capitalists: and then capital will receive better treatment. Labour, on the contrary, must always be found in a subordinate position, the number of consumers always and necessarily, in individual concerns, exceeding that of the labourers; such a position may be in some slight degree improved by circumstances, but it must yet be always secondary, dependent, labour being outside the centre of the enterprise. . . . . . In the English societies it was natural for this to happen . . . . .

This "robbing" of labour by means of these co-operative unions, which had announced their desire to inaugurate a new era of prosperity and well-being for the working-classes, discouraged many co-operators in England and excited derisive laughter against the "poet co-operators." Co-operators, on the other hand, resolved to remedy this painful state of affairs, and thus arose "the question of manufacturing societies."

The contest, which in England has lasted twelve years, between the societies which profit by this "robbing" and co-operators who vote that it be stopped, did not end even with the resolution taken in the Dewsbury Congress (May, 1888), which advised all distributing societies generally, and "wholesales" in particular, in the interests of the society, to assign a share of the profits to the labourers.[1] In pursuance of this vote a circular was despatched from the central co-operative office to all distributing societies, questioning them on their relations with the "productive departments," and pointing out the vote of the congress. Out of all the societies questioned, only 199 responded—of these 138 declared that they had no productive departments, and 61 replied more or less fully to the circular. To the demand, "ought the society to admit working-men, employed productively in it, to share in the product," 5 replied in the affirmative, 46 in the negative.

[1] Schloss in an article—*Labour Problem (Fortnightly Review,* 1889)—points out as the principal causes of the London Dock Strike, which lasted from August 13th to September 14th, 1889, the small extent of manufacturing co-operative societies and of participation in the profits of productive enterprises.

After such a result as this many declared it was impossible to solve this problem.

But the impossible, writes Holyoake,[1] the veteran apostle of English co-operation, with youthful enthusiasm, has been achieved in Scotland: at Shieldhall, the productive department of the Glasgow "wholesale," the workmen employed have a large share in the profits, and some receive twenty per cent. more than the operatives working in other Glasgow manufacturing firms. It is true that participation in the product is only an imperfect form of co-operation, and a step still remains from this to the true manufacturing co-operative society, but it is no less true that the Shieldhall precedent, which, it may be hoped, will not be an isolated one, teaches that "robbery" of the workmen is not an absolute logical necessity in distributing societies, but where there exists a high degree of moral and intellectual education, the selfishness of consumers may well be tempered and brought into harmony with the interests of the workmen, of the whole.

In another way, not purely ideal, distributing societies may directly assist manufacturing co-operative societies, reconciling their opposing interests and securing a sale for them: thus the Asti Co-operative Society sells crockery ware and glass produced by the two co-operative societies of Imola and Altare, saving,

[1] *Co-operative News*, September, 1889.

in the interest of consumers, the gains of wholesale merchants by going straight to the manufacturers.

Even where there does not exist, as yet, a sufficient moral and intellectual standard to allow of the reconciliation of every interest of these two forms of cooperation, the distributing can always assist the manufacturing society by moral and material support —it can procure credit and capital for it. For instance, the labourers' societies of the Romagne would not be much concerned how to exist if, in our country, distributing societies on the English system had been widely diffused so as to place at the disposal of these societies a share of capital which capitalists, from a want of confidence, are unwilling to grant. Naturally, the subsidising of these societies is not unattended with risk to distributing societies, and it is well therefore to exercise the greatest caution.

From the most recent evidence, of which a brief account has been given, Rabbeno's opinion seems to me as exaggerated as Gide's: Rabbeno's is exaggerated, because he believes that any co-operative relationship between distributing and manufacturing societies is impossible, and Gide's exaggerated as trusting in a harmonious agreement between the one and the other form of co-operation. Gide, indeed, exaggerates this idea of his to the bounds of Utopia, saying as he does that since distributing societies are for the benefit of consumers, and all men are consumers, to assist these societies is, as it were, to promote the general happiness. But, on the contrary, it may be asserted that, if all men are, on pain of death, consumers, they are not therefore *only* consumers. The majority of them—excluding, that is to say, the parasites of society—contribute to production: and if consumption is the object of production, it does not, as all social economy teaches, follow that there is perfect harmony between the one and the other.

CHAPTER VIII.

SOME OBSERVATIONS ON THE THEORY OF CO-OPERATION.

In defining the economic idea of co-operation, which differs from speculation and beneficence, perplexity has been the lot of all those persons who refer every economic phenomenon to two moral causes—egoism and altruism (to use pretty modern expressions)—to which all those actions, performed for a speculative or philanthropic purpose, evidently correspond. But the moral motives which variously determine human activity, and form the ultimate causes of economic phenomena, may be not only egoist and altruist, but also mutualist, and co-operation is based precisely on this last. The bond which unites the members of a co-operative society is not founded on pure individual egoism, however much the co-operative society may, as an individual body, act egoistically towards third parties. Mutualism is precisely the premiss of all those aggregations with a moral object which are not of a purely egoist origin, in which, that is to say, each member, aiming, indeed, at his own ecomomic advantage, limits himself to obtaining a smaller advantage than he would desire, if he were actuated by egoism pure and simple.

Nor does this assertion contradict the latest doctrine by which the real ultimate premiss of economic facts is the supreme principle of the fewest means. The principle of the fewest means which may be applied when the object of economic activity is egoistic and altruistic, may be applied also when the object is mutualist;[1] and when the form of co-operation represents the fewest means for attaining a given economic end, we have an application of this mutualism.

On this mutualism, besides those forms of co-operation properly so-called, are based other forms of economy, such as assurance and mutual aid societies; which imply an exchange of services and loans between the members for one specific object. Hence it will be well to bring out some points of difference between those forms.

In assurance societies, as is patent and obvious in mutual societies, it is in fact the union of the assured which assures itself, *i.e.*, every person assured in them is also an assurer, and, to use the phrase of the venerable Samuel Best, one member in these societies must bear the burden of another; but while the object of assurance is thus to lighten economic losses brought about by misfortune, *i.e.*, by uncertain events, the

[1] De Viti de Marco, *Carattere economico dell' economia finanziaria*, 1888, p. 48 *et. seqq.*—Sax, *Grundlegung der theoretischen Staatswirthschaft*, Vienna, 1887, p. 148 *et seqq.*

object of co-operation is to procure for the members a material advantage which is both constant and independent of external accidents. While the one has a negative action—that of lessening the consequences of a loss which has befallen one member by distributing the burden among all the members—the other, on the contrary, has a positive action, that of procuring a direct advantage for all the members.

Still greater differences exist between co-operative and mutual aid societies and, generally, those institutions which combine the advantages of assurance and collective saving. In truth, while mutual aid societies are for the exclusive benefit of members, co-operative societies may extend their action to non-members. Besides, whilst the latter exclude all assistance (patronage) on the part of the well-to-do, this is nearly always found in mere provident institutions.

Just as the sentiment of mutualism was frequently defined as that which is neither altruist nor egoist, so sometimes co-operation was defined as a form of economy which is different alike from speculation and beneficence; there being thus indicated only the negative idea of co-operation. Afterwards many who believed they were giving a positive definition, frequently confined themselves to an emphatic enumeration of the benefits and aims of co-operation, and thus avoided a real definition.[1]

[1] Here are some examples. I. Cantu (*Mutualità e coopera-*

It is only lately that striking definitions have been given. Wollemberg[1] has defined co-operation as the "spontaneous organisation of a number of particular economies, dominated by a common need, for exercising collectively and independently the industrial function which produces the specific economic loans adapted to satisfy it." In this notion, observes Rabbeno,[2] the idea of co-operation is very well ex-

zione, Milano, 1871) writes : " Co-operative societies have as their reason, fraternity; their principle, equality; their means, the honour, probity and labour of associated co-operators : and as their object the emancipation of all."

James Thomson defines co-operation as an association of workers for the purpose of procuring for themselves, by the greatest economy, the means of satisfying the needs of existence and of improving their moral, intellectual, physical and social condition by an equal division and prudent distribution of the profits of their labour.

Marshall in the inaugural address of the twenty-first congress of English co-operators, instead of defining co-operation, restricts himself to calling it "the typical product of our age." Truly the products which are described as typical of our age are now so numerous, that that which is really such can no longer be found.

Hubert Valleroux (N. Dictionnaire d'écon-polit, edited by L. Say, Paris, 1890, at the word association) writes gaily of co-operative societies that, "l'usage e donné ce nomme à des sociétés assez différents entre elles et qui n'ont de commun que d'avoir été fondées assez récemment et par application d'une même idée," while it is just this même idée which ought to be indicated.

[1] La teoria della cooperazione (Giornale degli economisti, vol. ii., fasc. ii., 1887).

[2] Società di produzione, Milano, 1889.

plained, but one thought is wanting in it, and that is that "the function exercised collectively serves to satisfy the needs only of those exercising it."

Rabbeno's addition, if it agrees with the uncomfortable results at which that excellent author arrives from the study of facts, and reveals his discouragement and disillusion with regard to co-operative ideals, does not seem to be necessary in a definition. In the definition of an idea which is ever assuming new and different applications, it is necessary to avoid those specifications which are proper to determinate conditions of time and place, but are extrinsic to the essential idea. Participation in the profits, introduced for the first time at Shieldhall by a distributing society, presents an example in which Rabbeno's addition would not be applicable, for in this case the distributing society not only satisfies the needs of consumers, in whose interest the society was founded, but the needs of other groups of individuals also. If it is true that Rabbeno's idea ordinarily corresponds with practice, it is not, therefore, true that it is always carried into effect and, therefore, ought to be omitted in a definition.

To Wollemberg's definition, which has certainly not the merit of brevity, I much prefer the definition of Dr. Emilio Cossa, according to which co-operation is the *exercise of determinate economic activities on the part of a number of persons who assume them for their common profit.*[1] From this definition the chief economic character of co-operative association becomes manifest, *i.e.*, that of being essentially a collection of persons, not of capital, or, as others have said, an association of consumers which derives its origin from common personal needs, and is carried into effect by the mutual interchange of personal services, through the presence in the participators of determinate aptitudes. Moreover, this definition in the phrase " for their common profit "—for which the author, in his lectures at the Pavia Athenæum, has fitly substituted " *in order to satisfy a common need* "—without adding the note " exclusively," which Rabbeno desires, delineates more securely the idea of co-operation.

Rabbeno, after unfolding the idea of co-operation, observes that this idea, as a general form of economic organisation, is at bottom a socialist idea, as implying a collective economy in which all functions would be exercised collectively, all needs satisfied collectively, and the persons and interests of producers and consumers would not be distinguished, but the whole economy would be organised in view of the common needs of all.

But can it be properly stated that the co-operative movement is a socialist movement?

Before all, it is said that co-operation must naturally be a socialist institution, having been developed in

[1] Op. Cit. p. 116.

consequence of Owen's attempts at socialism—the daughter cannot have degenerated from the father. But, instead of having fallen off, might not the daughter have improved, as compared with the father, as, for instance, chemistry, which is the child of alchemy? Further, it may be observed that the ideal of some socialists, of Kirkup,[1] for example, is precisely a well-organised and complete co-operative system, of which the present state of co-operation is only a partial application. "Great principles," he writes, "cannot be carried out all at once, but require long preparation, through graduated changes, in an infinity of particulars sufficiently prosaic, in order that they may be perfectly applied."

And I have already drawn attention to the fact that the Belgian co-operative movement is, in a large measure, the work of socialists, however much socialism may have given to it a particular tendency; which at once shows that socialism and co-operation are not one and the same idea. That the co-operative does not correspond with the socialist ideal may be proved also by calling to mind the expression of the French socialist workmen, whereby *la coopération démoralise les ouvriers en faisant des bourgeois*, and the declaration of the Red Internationals in the United States, to whom every form of co-operation is

[1] Thomas Kirkup, *An Enquiry into Socialism*. London, 1887.

despicable, because it is a palliative which postpones the time of the final emancipation of workmen.

In Germany, also, the co-operative does not coincide with the socialist ideal, and the *Volkstribune*, in which Liebknecht and Bebel write, asked quite recently whether socialists were not wrong in opposing the co-operative movement, and whether it was not better to repent of such an error. And in Italy, in the Romagne, it was lately observed with joy that not a few socialist workmen, especially after the foundation of the labourers' society, were gradually converted to co-operation.

In reality, the co-operative ideal is neither socialist nor conservative: strict socialists and conservatives, differing in every particular, agree in the common desire to beat down co-operation, since for the one party it implies a peaceable and not a violent emancipation, while for the other it has always the sin of implying the emancipation of the people. Neither does State socialism—the doctrine of *Staatshülfe*—whereby it is desired to favour and promote co-operative societies by public initiative, impress a socialist character on co-operation: at present, on the contrary, the bad results which have been yielded by this State intervention, especially in Germany and France, and the evident advantage, confirmed by practice, of following the lead of private individuals—a course warmly supported by Schulze-Delitzsch in his diatribes against Lassalle—have caused in Europe and America the just and liberal opinion to prevail, that co-operative societies ought to ask nothing of the State, except that liberty to develop themselves be not taken from them.

In any case, if any one desires to call co-operation socialist—co-operation, the most admirable form of self-help, in which the progress of all is facilitated, since each one, as he rises himself, assists his comrade to rise; a form of economy which is not authoritative, does not sacrifice aught of liberty or individual rights, and which, moreover, does not suppose for its realisation men of a different nature from the present, inasmuch as it is based on the human character or spirit as it really is or may easily in the future become—certainly it will not be the stigma of socialism that will cause those fervent and patient co-operators to recoil who, with calm and vigorous action, know how to work, with a happy faith in the future, for the good of themselves and of society.

THE END.

www.ingramcontent.com/pod-product-compliance
Lightning Source LLC
Chambersburg PA
CBHW020238170426
43202CB00008B/126